Mallie Stafford

The March of Empire Through Three Decades

embracing sketches of California history, early times and scenes, life in the mines,

travels by land and sea before the era of railroads

Mallie Stafford

The March of Empire Through Three Decades
embracing sketches of California history, early times and scenes, life in the mines, travels by land and sea before the era of railroads

ISBN/EAN: 9783337272920

Printed in Europe, USA, Canada, Australia, Japan

Cover: Foto ©ninafisch / pixelio.de

More available books at **www.hansebooks.com**

THE
MARCH OF EMPIRE

THROUGH THREE DECADES.

EMBRACING

Sketches of California History;

EARLY TIMES AND SCENES; LIFE IN THE MINES; TRAVELS BY LAND AND SEA BEFORE THE ERA OF RAILROADS; THE EAST DURING THE YEARS OF THE CIVIL WAR; LIFE IN THE BORDER STATES; CROSSING THE PLAINS WITH OX TEAMS; CROSSING THE PLAINS ON THE TRANSCONTINENTAL RAILWAY; PROGRESS AND IMPROVEMENT OF THE GOLDEN STATE; RESOURCES; ETC., ETC.

BY

MRS. MALLIE STAFFORD.

SAN FRANCISCO:
GEO. SPAULDING & CO., GENERAL PRINTERS, 414 CLAY STREET.
1884.

TO THOSE

WHO WERE EVER MY WARM FRIENDS, ALIKE IN SUNSHINE

AND IN SHADOW,

THIS LITTLE VOLUME IS MOST AFFECTIONATELY

DEDICATED.

PREFACE.

In response to many requests of friends and acquaintances, I have copied from the tablets of memory a brief recital of adventures which occurred during thirty years of wanderings in the West, mingling it with scraps and sketches of history. The author feels a natural timidity in presenting her personal experiences to the public, but hopes it may prove of sufficient interest to warrant a perusal, the object being to preserve, along with many other and worthier works, a remembrance of those old-time customs, scenes, modes of traveling, etc., which belong essentially to the past, and which are fast disappearing in reality, as also from memory.

To those who have participated in the stirring scenes of early days in California and the Western border, it is to be hoped this little volume will recall many similar adventures and pleasurable events; and to the general reader and the young, to whom these accounts are but as scraps of remote history and bygone times, it is my earnest hope that this brief recital will prove a faithful mirror, which will reflect the peculiar scenes and adventures connected with the dawn of civilization in the West

THE MARCH OF EMPIRE.

CHAPTER I.

INTRODUCTORY.

Looking back over the long, eventful trail of nearly thirty years, how distinctly one recalls to memory the fabulous stories of gold discovered on the Pacific Coast and the wild excitement they created; the smile of derision with which they were received by some, but with belief and faith by the many. And how vividly returns to mind the visions of long trains of emigrant wagons, that, winding slowly westward, moved out of the border cities, laden with their rich freight of human beings—men, women and tender children—bound for the country of their aspirations, California—the land to which so many longing eyes were hopefully cast, the Mecca to which thousands of pilgrims bent their daring and adventurous steps, and the shrine of many a splendid dream and gilded hope!

How well those ambitious dreams and gilded hopes were realized, the years have given us answer. Out of the then indiscernible and hidden future, time has enrolled chapter upon chapter of our young State's dazzling history; a history that is replete with the daring deeds, heroic acts, privations and adventures of her early pioneers. The civilization and cultivation of the golden Occident is due to the brain, muscle and sterling principles of her early pioneers. To them the country was an almost unbroken wilderness, over whose rich but uncultivated valleys roamed herds of cattle and horses, and peopled by a rude, barbaric race. Unskilled and ignorant, and unambitious, they dreamed away an idle and listless existence—unenviable, indeed, save for its luxurious content.

But the discovery of gold, in 1848, opened up a new era on the Pacific slope, and immigration poured in by sea and land. It is the old story of how thousands left their cheerful firesides; left friends, kindred, wives, little ones, and all that centres in that sweet word *home*, and with the new, unexplored gold fields of California in view, they braved the terrors of the sea, the long voyage around the "Horn" and the dread malaria of the tropics; or, "crossing the plains," they braved "dangers seen and unseen" in the wild and trackless wilderness, over swollen rivers and across snowy mountains. Ever in danger of an attack from the hordes of merciless savages that lined their path, they toiled onward, often without guide, and nothing save the compass and their trust in God to direct them to the land of their hopes. Alas! how many "faltered by the wayside," and, weary, found a rest in an unknown grave by the flowing river, in the dim sands of the desert, or under the pines on the mountain's brow. Perhaps it is in consequence of the dangers and hardships endured, and the success which attended their efforts, that a sort of lofty pride mantles the brow of the gray-haired pioneer as he recounts in thrilling tones the adventures which befel his party when he "crossed the plains" in the Spring or Summer of '49. The lustre of that pride which glows with a just fervor in the heart of the pioneer of the forties, is felt, though perhaps more dimly, in the breast of the immigrant of the fifties. It is, therefore, with a feeling of pleasure that I review a part of that early history; that I look back over a portion of the long, eventful trail—a portion, too, of the trail that is fast becoming obliterated by new innovations. "Crossing the plains" with ox teams, which journey required a period of nearly six months, and "rounding the Horn" in a sailing vessel, are remembered now as events that belong essentially to the past. They have passed into history along with the Digger Indian, the Spanish vaquero and the old adobe building, and things and scenes associated with and a part of the introductory pages of our still young, but rapidly developed State.

No more the long, unbroken trains
   Of ox teams on the desert sands,
Bear onward, in the creaking wains,
   The emigrant in weary bands.

The years that passed! the years that passed!
   Bear witness to unwritten tales
And histories; for along the vast
   Dim trackless sands and winding vales,
Once stirred, in Life's quick throbbing beat,
The tramp of many thousand feet.

They live with us, those years that made
   Our young athletic State unfold
Her hidden powers of wealth, and laid
   Her history in an age of gold.

And we, a part of that great throng,
   Who bravely stemmed the threat'ning waves—
Or trackless waste, that all along
   Was thickly marked with new made graves;—
Oh! we cannot forget the old
   Long journeys to the "Land of Gold."

To-day the shining track of steel
   Stretches from East-land to the West.
We sit in gliding car and feel
   The idle luxury of rest—
And templed cities, vast and fair,
   Pass by like phantoms on the air.

But O! our hearts cannot forget
   The past—that is a part of us:
Those long remembered times, which yet
   Are sacred as the half-buried dust
Of those, who fainting found a rest
   In the wild deserts of the West.

CHAPTER II.

THE DEPARTURE — EVENINGS ON SHIP-BOARD — SALT WATER BATH — GREEN ISLAND OF CUBA — CENTRAL AMERICA — THE NATIVE WOMEN — CASTILIAN LADIES.

In a fair city of the west, one lovely morning in October in 1854, there was gathered at the depot a group of friends. It was the occasion of my departure for California in company with my husband, on the eastward bound train for New York. Looking backward over the dim trail, grass-grown and half obscured by the crowding events and wonderful changes since that time, I find myself wondering if indeed I am the same being, the same, who almost thirty years ago, amid a vast throng of fellow-voyagers, was outward bound for the new country of golden dreams.

Time passes quickly enough; but looking back through all these years, and briefly summing up the changes. the vast achievements of science, the progress and improvements in the history of nations, the wonderful inventions and remarkable discoveries, and the grand opening up of the western half of our continent, it would seem that ages and ages had written its intelligible hieroglyphics on the world's history. So rapidly have these events succeeded each other, that in going back in retrospection over the old familiar landmarks, I brush aside the foliage, and remove the dense undergrowth as I attempt to reveal some of the scenes and events of those long past years.

That bright October morning! There was that peculiar perfume in the atmosphere suggestive of early frosts. There was that dreamy haze which gives to the sunshine a softer tint, the beautiful haze of Indian summer. The hills were crowned with sumach, wild grape vines, etc., and were arrayed in all the crimson glory of early autumn. And as our train sped swiftly on, we drank in the sweet breezes that came from the low woodlands—saw the fields of rustling corn bending underneath their freight of tawny grain, the lark, soaring in mid air, carrolled to us a glad goodby, and farm houses, cities and villages passed in rapid succession. Having reached New York, the grand American metropolis, with its endless, busy streets, filled with a surging mass of human beings—and after spending a few days in sight-seeing, we purchased tickets for the P. M. S. S. Co. line, and were soon on board the staunch steamer *North Star*, running between New York and Aspinwall. The black cloud-like vapor issuing from the smoke-stack, tells us that she will ere long be on her voyage; and soon there is the hurry and commotion of departure, the creaking of machinery, groaning of the engines, rattling of cordage, and amid it all the hoarse commands of officers. With the rapid farewell of friends, the waving of hats and handkerchiefs, we are out upon the bay and steaming down the Sound, and feel that we have launched our bark on the broad ocean, have sundered old ties, parted from the country of our birth, from friends and old associates and familiar scenes—and with what thronging emotions did I stand and watch the dim receding strand, and saw in the distance through the blue vapor of that bright October morning, the forms I loved, and waving hands.

There is always something indescribably sad in parting from those we love; but a parting like this!—to see the blue waves close over the shining track of the vessel, to watch the fast-fading shore and see around us the great world of waters, is doubly solemn. We had on board nine hundred passengers, but amid the hurry and excitement of the first few hours out at sea I stood alone, feeling that sinking of the heart as I watched the shore of my native land recede from sight. Going on deck the next morning, I strained my eager vision to the right, but there was not the faintest shadow of the land, not the most cloud-like semblance visible on the far horizon. Around us, on either hand, rolled the blue, restless waves of the Atlantic.

It was then that we realized that we were indeed launched on the vast world of waters. How limitless it appeared, as it rolled, billow upon billow, till lost in the far distance it vanished on the rim of the clear horizon. At such a time, and such a place, how forcibly are we reminded of our own feebleness and our utter dependence on the Supreme Being—He who spake worlds into existence, and guides the ship through the trackless ocean. At such a time, in such a place, we are prone "'To own the littleness of man; the mightiness of God." There is inherent in the soul of every human being a worshipful tendency, a tendency to own and acknowledge the grandeur and goodness of the Maker of the Universe; but soiled by contact with the world and long wandering from the fold of the Good Shepherd, like wayward children, we often forget His loving presence, and worship new idols; but brought face to face with His grandest creations we cannot but acknowledge and bow in adoration before the great First Cause. What though we are led away by "vain philosophies" and false speculations, beyond and over it all we know that *God reigns*. It was such a thought, unuttered but felt, that stirred my soul as I stood gazing out on the grandeur, the fearful sublimity of the ocean, and thought of the perils and hardships "of those who go down to the sea in ships." My spirits, young, light and elastic, soon became accustomed to the novelty and grandeur of the scene that daily met my view. It was my delight to take my seat at the prow of the vessel, and watch with tireless pleasure the ship, as it rose and fell with the motion of the waves, now up above the foaming waters while the stern was deep in the trough of the sea, and then reversed, I was let down and down until my outstretched hand could almost reach the boiling billows. Few ladies attempted this feat, and often I was warned by the sailors and officers that if I remained there I would get seasick, but it was my good fortune never to be troubled with that disagreeable sensation. As days passed we formed some pleasant acquaintances, it being a recognized endeavor to try to make the time pass as pleasantly as possible; so life on shipboard proved, though rather irksome, to be one long holiday, in which one is released from the set rules and toils and cares of existence. On such a voyage warm friendships are often formed that last through the eventful mazes of a lifetime, but in this one instance it is somewhat singular that of all that vast company with whom we journeyed, with whom we laughed and sang and parted on the golden shore, I have since met but one. Doubtless they, like ourselves, have wandered in devious paths, have floated with the ever-restless tide of the times, have followed the phantom, till weary of the search, are content at last to find a home in some sequestered vale or mountain slope.

Evenings on shipboard were particularly delightful. Gathered on the deck in little groups, we whiled the long hours away in pleasant conversation, rehearsing stories and singing songs, the music floating out and blending with the murmur of the waves. At other times the blue Atlantic—often variable and fretful—rolled its great waves and rocked our strong ship as a cradle. It was on such occasions that most of the passengers sought their berths, and, assuming a reclining position, endeavor to keep down their rising—breakfast, dinner or supper. There was then a noticeable falling off at table; a sort of let-me-alone-if-you-please expression on the woeful faces of the afflicted ones. Not infrequently some thoughtless passenger neglected to close the port-hole of his state-room, and the sea, suddenly rising, drenched him from head to foot. I was on one occasion the thoughtless victim of a salt water bath.

While reclining one day in my berth, rocked by the motion of the vessel, and for want of better amusement, watching the changing position of everything movable—hats tumbling from their racks, carpet sacks and baskets sliding and careening across the floor, and boxes, bottles, etc., slipping, thumping and rolling hither and thither, there was a momentary darkening of my window, and as I turned to look, a deluge of the "blue and boundless" drenched me from head to foot. I uttered a scream, and to add to my "ten or fifteen different emotions," I was greeted by a hearty peal of laughter. As soon as I could clear my vision of the "briny deep," I recognized my next-door neighbor, who was hanging on to my door and laughing heartily at my moist, unpleasant appearance. It was what the sailors called a "heavy sea," and I thought so, too; but laughing is catching, and as the sea continued rough, I had not many days to wait to repay my neighbor in her "own coin." One day while standing at her door talking, she and her little girl being in her berth, there was a sudden lurch of the vessel, a grating sound, and then—whizz! swish! down came an abundant shower of old Neptune, completely covering for a moment mother and child. I could have laughed *revengefully*, only the poor, little babe presented such a pitiable picture as it clung to the wet garments of its mother.

Days passed, and one fine morning we saw dimly on our left, rising proudly out of the sea, the green island of Cuba. It was crowned with verdure, a very queen of the ocean; the waters were calm, rippling along its low, bright shore.

> O, isles that shine! O, isles that shine!
> Across the blue Carribean sea,
> I seem to see their faint sea-line
> Whose silver strand my spirit binds
> By far-off dreams of memory.

But steaming past, we are soon out of sight of the beautiful vision, and soon after we beheld the cloud-like outlines of a coast, and drifting outward and floating past us were stray planks, bark, seaweed and the floating debris of the shore, all harbingers of joy to the weary voyager. Soon the shore became less phantom-like and more distinct, and we sniffed the sweet land breeze, and felt with rapture that we were nearing the far-stretching shores of Central America.

Ere long our noble ship lay moored at the long wharf of Aspinwall, and we gathered up, amid the general hurry and commotion, our traveling equipments, and as we stepped on the unfamiliar shore felt, indeed, that our feet pressed foreign soil. There to our right stood a group of palm trees, drooping and picturesque, and lo! "beneath the palm trees' leafy shade," there lounged and idled a group of natives. In the peculiar costume of the bronzed sons of the tropics, they lazily watched the disembarking of the passengers. If we had imagined that the town itself would present a foreign appearance, that the houses would be built in the hacienda, adobe veranda style, we were mistaken. The long rows of hastily erected wooden buildings, generally one story high, were essentially modern and American, at least the business portion. But the inhabitants were all shades of color, the natives ranging from the light brown to the swarthy copper color, and merging into the sleek jet-black Jamaica negro, black as imagination can paint him; for him I entertained a sort of respect, as it was evident he was *pure blood*, but for the mixed element one could scarcely imagine his nationality, being to all appearances a little of everything colored.

The native women, with immense woven baskets poised on their heads, filled with oranges, pineapples, bananas, cocoanuts, plantains, and other tropical fruits, with Mexican cakes, meat, etc., thronged the streets vending their wares. In striking contrast to them were the Castilian ladies of the upper classes, who might be seen on balconies and verandahs, reclining in easy chairs and hammocks, enjoying a "*dolce far niente*" sort of existence. Lithe and graceful of figure, and fair of face, their long black curls swept over their shoulders in lustrous negligence, while with unceasing motion they swayed their fans. Did you ever observe with what fascinating grace of motion the Spanish beauty handles her fan? A languid undulating grace of motion that is at once the envy and despair of the Northern belle, and that is entirely in harmony with the indolent luxurious characteristics of the climate—the rich, warm, ease-loving tropics.

CHAPTER III.

A RIDE ON MULE-BACK—THE MOUNTING COMMENCED—SCENES AND INCIDENTS—CROSSING THE ISTHMUS.

At the time of which I write, the Central American railroad across the Isthmus had not been completed, and rumors of a ride on muleback to complete the journey had reached our ears. Novel pictures of this portion of the journey were portrayed in glowing colors—of steep and rocky defiles in the mountains; of dark, swift rivers to be crossed; deep, gloomy marshes to be forded—and all on muleback. The bare recital was enough to make the stoutest feminine heart quail with apprehension.

Shortly before train time, my husband went to a store and purchased for me a pair of calfskin boots—boys' boots. It was generally understood that there was going to be "fun ahead"—maybe trouble—and we deemed it best to be ready for any emergency. Those who had crossed the route before were well aware that it was advisable to be "booted" if not spurred for the occasion.

At six o'clock in the morning the warning whistle of the train sounded, and amid the rush, tumult and excitement, nine hundred passengers — "more or less," as the lawyers say — armed to the teeth with knapsack, overcoats, umbrellas, babies, poodles, guns, bird-cages — everything portable — went flying to the cars, bearing down upon the train like "an army with banners."

There was the French woman, with her poodle; the tall, angular hunter, with his gun; the old maid, with her bird-cage; the Dutch woman, with her four children, *and* her pair of twins in her arms; and there was—yes, there was, without doubt — the little woman with the calfskin boots, and when the engine shrieked, the bell rang and the train moved out from the foreign American-built city of the tropics, there was a general smoothing down of ruffled plumages, and with faces aglow with perspiration and excitement, we prepared to enjoy a flying glimpse of the scenery, etc. We cross bridges and span broad rivers and dark marshes, and rumble through deep gloomy forests, and faintly catch glimpses of thick trailing vines. heavy jungles and beautiful trees. Near noon we arrive at the terminus of the railroad—a small collection of shanties, bamboo huts, etc. A short time is allowed for dinner and to make preparations for the mule ride, a distance of twelve miles yet intervening between the terminus of the railroad and Panama.

A few restaurants, mere temporary affairs, are kept here by the natives—no very elaborate bill of fare. We enter one and call for dinner. We are motioned to a dark greasy-looking table, innocent of cloth, and a tall, very yellow-tinted Spanish woman, with long black curls, silently fries some ham and eggs, which, with some black coffee supplemented by a plate of Mexican cakes, comprises the entire bill of fare, one dollar per meal. Strengthened and invigorated, we feel ready for the twelve-mile ride. If we are to believe as truth the stories which have reached us of the dangers and hardships, and in some cases, terrible adventures which have befallen many on this mule trail, we may well be pardoned for being apprehensive. What terrors and dangers may not lurk in the depths of yon dark forest, where the trail enters clear and distinct, but is soon swallowed up in the dense foliage and thick jungle! Close at hand is a large corral, into which has been driven an immense drove of mules. The passengers are now allowed to go and select their animals. Though the mule-ride is included in our through ticket, those who have crossed the Isthmus before are aware that by giving the natives in charge a few dollars extra he can select his mule from the band In this way it was my good fortune to get for my riding animal a fine large gray mule—"yes," says a lady at my elbow, "the very same one I rode over, just three months before." A short time previous to this, there had been a terrible massacre of Americans as they crossed the Isthmus, and according to the custom of the times and also apprehensive of trouble, most of the passengers were well armed. For this reason it was deemed advisable to start on the trail all together. The mules all being selected, the mounting commenced.

There was the big, fat woman to be provided with a mule, and the "heavy city father,'" of aldermanic proportions, and it was a singular fact that, as a rule, these big, fat people invariably had the misfortune, and I may say mortification, of getting the small, lean, jack-rabbit mule. It is a noticeable fact, that in almost every instance these immense people never get things in proportion to their size. With what anxiety and misgivings did they view the situation ! And how carefully did they mount and deposit their ponderous weight on the backs of the trembling, patient brutes !

"Oh, I know I shall never get there alive !"

said a bulky lady, as she towered over her thin little donkey, There also were ladies who had never been on horseback in their lives, and to whom the sight of a mule—a " horrid mule "—was enough to drive them mad. That they had to mount the horrid creatures, and be jostled and shaken—perhaps shaken off, was an idea too preposterous to be entertained. To add to it all, in "those good old times" we had no side-saddles—not on the mule trail. The style of riding advised by our male escorts was the style in vogue long before the invention of side-saddles, and much as we disliked to adopt the masculine mode of riding, we found before we had proceeded far both the wisdom and safety of it. Partly through timidity and partly through humiliation, several of the ladies demurred, and then refused to ride at all; some were crying as though their hearts would break, others were angrily scolding, and it required some time before they could be convinced that they *must* ride, since it was impossible to walk. Such a scene! Nine hundred passengers mounting nine hundred mules, with their various and multifarious equipments, belongings and encumbrances, the average being a roll of blankets strapped on behind, two carpet-sacks on the pummel of the saddle, and a large overcoat, shawl, bird cage, basket, umbrella, etc., which was carried in front. One may well imagine that under this nondescript load the little mule was lost to sight—not entirely—his ears, like Banquo's ghost, "would not down," but, true to nature, pointed with unerring fidelity to some imaginary degree in the zenith, assuring the traveler that he was a living reality. Mounted upon the hurricane deck of my noble gray, I sat an unobserved spectator, having accepted the inevitable with as good grace as I could command.

At last all being ready, we took up our line of march—"by twos and threes and single." Soon after entering the trail, it became necessary to go single file. Our little party, consisting of four or five ladies and eight or ten gentlemen, expressed a determination to try to keep together—a feat which might have been performed had it not been for the long trains of pack mules laden with freight, merchandise, baggage, etc., in charge of the dusky natives. Wherever an opportunity offered, the natives drove their pack trains ahead, and in among the passenger train, often separating friends and acquaintances. On one occasion a swarthy native in charge of a number of pack mules, in endeavoring to get ahead of me, drove them so closely against my mule as to nearly knock me off. Quick as thought, a voice behind me rang out, "What are you doing, you black rascal?" "Go to h—ll," defiantly shouted back the native. Immediately there was the click of a revolver, and turning I saw the gentleman, a fellow-passenger, with weapon drawn, was ready to fire. "Don't shoot, Thornton," said some one in front of me, "keep cool, don't shoot." The cap snapped, and the native having gone on, Thornton put up his revolver, when the gentleman in front proceeded to explain to the excitable Thornton the dangers of a serious affray with the natives on their own soil—"for," said he, "if you should happen to kill one of these black rascals, you would be tried by the Spanish authorities, and the probable result would be instant death, or at least languishing for years in a Spanish dungeon. The natives were bold and insolent, and constantly endeavoring to get their pack mules ahead of the passengers. They fully comprehended the advantages they possessed in being on their own soil, surrounded by their own countrymen, and did not fail to heap insults and indignities on defenseless Americans whenever they could get them in their power.

Although this novel and romantic part of the journey was beset with perils, inconveniences and annoyances, there were many things new and interesting to the lover of nature, and many incidents mirth-provoking and ludicrous. For a long distance the route lay through the heart of a deep dark jungle, so dense and thick that the sunshine scarcely ever penetrated it at midday. There were strange and beautiful trees, and clinging vines whose heavy weight hung down in a wealth of fruit and foliage. Far off the monkeys skipped and chattered from limb to limb of the tall trees; gay plumaged birds flitted in and out of the sombre woods, and one could imagine the reptiles and wild animals that doubtless infested the depths of the forest. When at length the character of the route changed, we ascended into a rocky and mountainous region, where for a long distance the trail led through a narrow defile in the mountains, affording only room enough for one animal to proceed, single file.

On each side a wall of rock rose perpendicularly many feet, as though a pass had been hewn through the solid rock; through this narrow defile, passengers and baggage trains slowly wended their way. The pack mules, loaded with boxes of merchandise, trunks, etc., not infrequently became wedged in in some uncommonly narrow place. This occasioned a halt of the whole party, and a jamming and squeezing until the mule could be liberated, which often was not accomplished until a native went around on top, threw ropes down which were fastened to the animal's load, and drew it up, thus freeing it. While riding along through this narrow defile, I looked ahead, and to my astonishment saw the passengers disappear as if they had suddenly sunk into the bosom of the earth, but on looking again I saw them reappear in the distance. My husband, who was a short distance in advance of me, turned, and giving me a look of stern command not unmingled with fear and desperation, forbade my further progress. "Go back, go back," said he, "don't come here;" just then he disappeared, and leaning forward I caught a glimpse of him at the bottom of what appeared to be a terrible precipice. I heard the heavy thud as the mule struck the ground, saw the carpet sacks shaken up, heard the jingling of the knives and forks in the lunch basket which he carried, and though peril and danger appeared imminent I could not repress a smile at the ridiculous picture presented—an indiscriminate mixture of mule, rider, carpet sacks, roll of blankets, lunch basket, etc.; but with an effort only equal to the emergency, the rider quickly adjusted himself and his belongings, and the mule, grave and solemn, proceeded on his way as though nothing had happened. If it had been instant death before me I could not have stopped, neither could I have turned around in the narrow pass; there was nothing for it but to cling on with all the strength I possessed. As we neared the descent, I noticed the mule pause for a brief second, and to my astonishment, he carefully placed his feet together in a little niche worn in the rocks and giving a spring like a dog, we were down altogether and safe. It gave us a terrible shaking up though, and in speaking of it afterwards, the tall, angular fellow from the backswoods remarked: "Well, sir, them thar mules does beat all natur fur bein' shore-footed; dang if they don't!" We concurred. How the fat people on the thin little donkeys, and the timid ladies stood the fearful leap, I leave it for the reader to imagine; for me that terror was past, and I was looking out for what was ahead. Being possessed of the rich heritage of youth, high health, courage and indomitable spirits, I thought little of the inconveniences, annoyances and even dangers to which we were exposed.

CHAPTER IV.

THROUGH A TROPICAL SWAMP — THE STUBBORN MULE — SEPARATED FROM FRIENDS — THE OLD RUINED FORT.

With the fearful leap we emerged from the narrow defile and entered a strip of low marshy land, which appeared to be a swamp, moist and muddy, the mud increasing until a perfect slush it reached half leg deep to the mules. Through this the long line of passenger and baggage trains slowly splashed. To add to the gloomy prospect, the rain—one never knows when to expect rain in that country—began to descend in a gentle mist. It was as if to remind us that a thing is "never so bad but it may be worse." Many a groan and imprecation, "not loud, but deep," escaped the lips of the jaded passengers. I was provided with a good wrap, and looking at my stout boots, I took courage. It proved, however, to be only a slight mist, and the sun was soon pouring down its scorching rays with all the intensity of that tropical climate. It came down fearfully hot as we slowly dragged, single file, through the slush of the swamp.

Presently an incident, interesting—nay, ludicrous—attracts the attention. Just in front of me is a very tall, harmless-looking fellow, mounted on a diminutive donkey. Beyond, in the neighboring forest, the monkeys kept up an incessant chattering, leaping from limb to limb of the strange trees. So engrossed had the tall man become with their exciting gambols that he did not notice the limb of a fallen tree that almost crossed his path. Soon his foot caught against the limb in such a manner that he could not extricate it without stopping. "Whoa!" said he, "Whoa, you dum fool! I say, whoa!" But the animal kept on, and—splash! thud! He had measured his length in the mire. He arose, with many a dire invective, the maddest and the muddiest, if not the wisest man I ever saw. A native stopped the mule long enough for him to remount. Such a sight! Mud from head to foot. One learned before getting to his journey's end that there is no use trying to stop a mule. When once his head is turned in a certain direction with a train, it is simply impossible for a stranger to stop or turn him from the old beaten track. With a stolid and persistent stubbornness, he turns neither to the right nor to the left, but keeps straight ahead, and *sabes* no English; but his quick and generous ear is instantly obedient to the native's "A moola! Hurra!" which, uttered with their peculiar intonation, seemed to be good mule language, and all that the exigencies of the case required. By degrees, and taking no note of our wanderings, we emerged into a broad and open thoroughfare, the macadamized road that leads some distance out from the old city of Panama. Like the old cathedrals and ruined forts, it appears to be a lingering landmark of an ancient civilization. Since leaving the narrow defile the natives had driven their pack trains ahead with greater energy, and on entering the road I found myself, with a small party of friends, separated by long trains of pack mules and their drivers from the main body of the passengers. As "coming events cast their shadows before," we knew by the scattering bamboo huts, which are occupied by the lowest and most depraved class of these people, that we would soon be in the environs of the city of Panama. Suddenly there was a stampeding of animals—exclamations in English, cursings in broken English and Spanish—and looking around, what was my horror to see that a large drove of pack mules, with their dusky drivers, had come in between me and my company, completely separating me from my friends, and in the din and general confusion I was being rapidly driven on with the pack train. While endeavoring vainly to make my companions answer my shouts, my attention was turned to my animal. There had appeared suddenly at my bridle bit, without noise and without warning, as if from the very center of the earth, a being who, for aught I knew, might be a denizen of the lower regions. Low-browed and sinister looking, his dark face had that hideous expression that one is apt to associate in imagination with the smell of sulphur and brimstone. He looked defiantly in my face, while with his right hand he kept a firm hold on my bridle bit. I was alone, and already out of sight of my friends! With a frantic effort I pulled up my animal, and commanded him, with flashing eyes, to "Let go of my bridle." He looked warily up and down the road, but still going on. Before and behind, for miles, it seemed, there was nothing to be seen but an endless train of pack mules and their dusky drivers. Still frantically pulling on my bridle, I saw that, with all my efforts, he was by degrees taking me from the pack train and from the main road, and entering a dim path that led down behind a deserted bamboo hut— and from there—where? With the energy of desperation, I made an effort to stop my animal, and shouted. "Let go of my bridle," and at the same time leaning forward, and aiming a blow across his bare shoulders with my riding whip; but he dodged the blow, and giving me a look full of sinister meaning, prepared to go on. The moment of delay, however, had been my salvation. As a last hope, I looked up the road, and with feelings of joy and gratitude I discerned, amid the dust and moving pack trains, a mounted figure. It was a horseman! He was galloping at full speed, and by his dress I knew him to be an American. "Thank God!" I murmured; and pointing with my whip, I said to the native, "My friends are coming." The rascal's keen eye had caught sight of the horseman, and he released his hold on my bridle. By this time the horseman was at my side. "Why, madam," said he, "you are losing your way. Are you alone?" "Yes," I replied, and immediately told him the whole story, trembling with excitement during its recital. I never get frightened until the danger is over, or at least these feelings so long held under control find expression, when we realize that we have passed though a danger, and we are safe. "But where is the native?" said the gentleman. We looked up and down, far and near, and lo! he had disappeared. As though the earth had opened and swallowed him, he was nowhere to be seen. I expressed some anxiety about my friends, and being alone. "Never fear," said he; "I'll see to your safety. I am a runner from the Louisiana Hotel in Panama, on my way to meet the passengers. They are doubtless not far behind." A large drove of pack animals was passing, their copper-colored drivers hoarsely shouting, "A moola! Hurra! Hurra!" and when the dust occasioned by them had drifted away, we saw in the distance the passenger train slowly coming into view. With many heartfelt thanks to the stranger, whose very name to this day is unknown to me, I rejoined my friends. But for his timely arrival, what might have been my fate? I shudder to think! Had some trivial circumstance delayed his coming five or ten minutes, I doubtless would not to-day be here, a living entity; would not be here writing by the open window, where the soft midsummer breeze steals gently through the vines, and the mystic music of the pines sings its changeful melody. On such a slender thread does human destiny so often hang!

Rumors were rife of many a dark and bloody deed that had been committed on this dangerous route. Men had been murdered for their money and clothing, and women had been stolen away and murdered for their jewelry. The natives appeared to be the lowest type of humanity, treacherous, malicious, deceptive and avaricious, many of them being capable of committing the foulest murder for a small sum of money. Only a few months before the natives, armed, had waylaid a train of passengers, and robbed and massacred them in open daylight. These dark and awful rumors still filled the air, and it was with feelings of gratitude and thankfulness that we arrived at the Louisiana Hotel in Panama, and took shelter under its hospitable roof. To one whose eyes had been accustomed to the onward march of civilization, and the giant strides of progress and modern improvements, this quaint and ancient Spanish city, crouching in listless apathy, like a grand old donna beside the sea, appeared a novel wonder. Like all foreign cities of any importance, it had its American or English quarter. Here was a street of hotels, restaurants, saloons, etc., but beyond were the dark adobe buildings and bamboo huts. Taking a ramble after supper, we paused in front of the dark and gloomy cathedral, which is built of sun-dried brick, its walls several feet thick, and covered with a tile roof. The ancient edifice looked as though it might have withstood the storms of centuries. Here knelt the Spanish devotee, clad in the light attire of the low classes of the tropics, and side by side with him came the high-born Donna and her maid. Before one shrine they knelt and offered up their aves to their patron saint.

An object of thoughtful interest was the old ruined fort, grass-grown and moss-covered, and crumbling beneath the weight of centuries. Its echoes responded now only to the whirr of the bat, the hoot of the owl, and the hiss of the venomous reptile; but it held in its massive walls many a dark and bloody history. What stirring tales of war, invasion and gallant defense did the crumbling pile suggest! But years had passed over its mouldering walls since the hand of silence had hushed the ring of its aforetime stormy echoes. Could the ghosts of those long and half-forgotten days arise, there would come forth from those ruined aisles and grass-grown walls, the ghosts of mail-clad Spanish heroes, whose deeds and deaths are linked with that remote period, and with the history of the old fort in the days of its ancient splendor.

It was scarcely considered safe for ladies to

be out on the streets at night, and though many of us might have enjoyed a stroll under the light of the moon in the quaint old town, and in the picturesque suburbs, and along its placid shores, we were forced to content ourselves as best we could at the hotels. My husband, however, in company with a fellow-passenger, took advantage of the beautiful moonlit night for a ramble. Save the light of the moon and the few lamps and candles in the business houses, the city was wrapt in gloom. Some impulse impelled them to direct their steps toward the old ruined fort. It was growing late, the streets were deserted, and silence and gloom brooded over the vicinity. As they neared the ruins, they caught the sound of female voices not far off. Hastening their steps the sounds became more distinct; it seemed to be voices in entreaty, mingled with sobbing and crying. "There's something wrong here," said one. "Let's hurry." A few steps farther, and in the dim half-light of the moon, they saw a native leading two mounted mules. As they approached, a voice rang out: "For Heaven's sake save us," "we want to go to the hotel, and this native is taking us we know not where." In a moment they were at their side, and demanding of the native where he was going with the ladies, at the same time attempting to take hold of the bridle, which the native held in his hand. Nothing daunted, the native defiantly drew a long knife, and uttering a curse prepared to defend his position. Enraged, one of the Americans presented his revolver and exclaimed, "If you don't leave here, I'll blow your brains out." The gleam of the revolver proved to be a powerful persuader, and the Mexican sullenly slunk back in the shadows. The ladies were the wife and daughter of the French Consul of San Francisco. When described to me, I remembered having often seen them on shipboard; they were remarkable for their large and handsome figures, and beautiful, clear complexions. They explained that they had become separated from their party and were late in getting in, and the native who had assumed charge of their animals was taking them *out* of the city, through the dark and gloomy suburbs. Doubtless their flashing jewelry and rich attire had been a strong temptation for the avarice of the Mexican, for the fact was apparent that he was *stealing them away*—where and for what purpose we were left to surmise. With tears and sobs they thanked their rescuers, who instantly conducted them to the hotel. Their friends, who had long been anxiously awaiting them, and wondering why they had not arrived, were overjoyed to receive them. This incident, added to my own personal experience convinced me that we had heard no idle rumors, that dark and mysterious deeds had been committed, and that "the half had not been told."

A heavy rain had fallen after our arrival, and towards evening a crowd of passengers came in, many of whom were soaking wet, a dejected looking set, tired and hungry, and even in that tropical country chilled through. Truly they looked as though "life was one long eternal washday," and that they had not only cast their colors in the conflict, but were ready to be hung up to dry. To add to their discomforts, all the extra clothing they had with them was wet, too, and their trunks — where were they? "Oh, if I only had my trunk!" was the prevailing sentiment; but one might as well have tried to probe the bottom of the sea for a pearl as to think of getting one's trunk under the circumstances. At such a time one keenly feels the uncertainty of all things terrestrial, especially a defenseless and hapless trunk that has taken, or is suppopsed to have taken, a ride over a wild, inhuman country on the back of a wild, irresponsible mule driven by a wild, demoralized, irrepressible son of the tropics. Ladies were scolding, crying, laughing, and many of the wisest ones were rapidly pacing up and down the parlors and verandahs "to keep up circulation" until they could get a change of clothing. Among them all one did not fail to notice those cheerful and sunshiny natures who, no matter how disagreeable the circumstances, always "make the best of it;" a determination not to let disagreeable circumstances rob them of enjoyment. They wait not for the gifts of fortune, for after all the best things we have in life are not what are thrown at our feet by the fickle hand of fortune, but rather what we gain by stern will and strong endeavor.

CHAPTER V.

THE BAY OF PANAMA — PREPARATIONS FOR EMBARKATION — THE SCENE ON THE BEACH — THE FLOWER OF MEXICAN CHIVALRY — BAY OF ACAPULCO.

The following morning dawned beautiful and bright. How lovely is early morning in the tropics! An early breakfast enabled us to take a stroll along the beach. This was the day of departure, and already the fine steamer *Golden Gate* lay anchored in the offing. The Bay of Panama is one of surpassing beauty. The gleaming shore, shell-strewn and even, slopes gently to the water's edge, reflecting in its transparent beauty rock, shells, islands and the myriad boats that float upon its surface. The bay abounds in islands, green and lovely, and almost burdened with a wealth of tropical verdure. Here are ornamental and pictueresque haciendas, owned and occupied by the wealthy Dons. Through field and meadow and pasture land roam their fat herds, and goats and sheep climb nimbly over the overhanging rocks, giving to the lovely picture an air of homelike beauty. In the offing lay moored numerous vessels—sailing ships, barks, steamships, etc.—and noticeable among them was a large British man-of-war. Her ponderous hull and ominous port-holes, from which could be distinctly seen the mounted cannon, frowned darkly over the green surface of the bay. How fragrant was the breeze, blown shoreward from the islands! It was perfumed with an aroma of spices, oranges, the sweet scent of the coffee tree, and the myriad odors of the productions of the fascinating tropics. Here everything suggests indolence, luxury, abundance, ease. No busy hum of trade and commerce, no stir and strife of progress and improvement disturbs the ease-loving natives. The poorer classes, as a rule, collect the mango, the cocoa, the yam, the plantain, and other wild fruits for their living—and for their dress—but this was a matter which seemed to be of minor importance to them, a yard of cotton cloth being generally sufficient for a full suit.

It was not long after sunrise before preparations for embarkation were made. The bay, gently sloping out to deep water for a distance of a hundred yards or more, was so shallow that even the small boats could not reach the shore.

How were we to traverse this intervening stretch of sea? With us there was no modern Moses, who with a wave of his rod could bid the waves roll back, and leave for our willing feet a dry roadway to the vessel. In my wanderings it had been my fortune to have been familiar with the various modes of travel known to christendom — steamship, steamboat, canal boat, flat boat, stage-ride, horseback, muleback — but the means necessary to be employed in order to reach the small boats was a "new departure" from any style of traveling which I had heretofore known. As the Central American native seems to be, to all intents and purposes, an amphibious animal, it was therefore necessary, as the only available expedient, to call into requisition his services for this important undertaking. Previous to this, many of the ladies had thought that a muleback ride comprised the realization of the horrible. What, therefore, must have been their despair when they saw that, in order to traverse that sheet of intervening sea, it was necessary — nay, unavoidable — to take that celebrated "post-back" ride with which all early Californians are acquainted, either through experience or rehearsal.

The scene on the beach was one never to be forgotten. It is photographed on my memory with imperishable fidelity. Beyond, in the offing, lay the grand steamer, her officers and crew busy in making preparations for a speedy departure. Near by were the small boats, manned by swarthy natives; and on the beach were crowds of passengers and piles of baggage and freight. Among them all moved the dusky, half-nude figures of the natives, intent on making as many ten-cent trips, the price of transportation, as possible. The outlook was anything but desirable. Anxious faces looked seaward, and trembling voices inquired if the boats could not be "got nearer." Ladies looked dismayed, and fat people, men and women, were in despair; but, whatever feelings of repugnance or fear we may have had to this novel mode of traveling, had to be thrust aside. It was one of the things inevitable, and the placid bay was soon disturbed by the lithe figures of the natives, bearing their novel burdens to the boats. What a medley of voices!—screaming and crying and laughing, not to chronicle any harsher expression of feeling. A thin, slender native offered his services to an aldermanic old gentleman. "Me pack Mericano—ten cent," said the native. "O, God bless me!" puffed the old gentleman, "I'm afraid—I'm afraid, my good fellow—I'm afraid you couldn't just stand up to it." "O, me pack—me pack," insisted the native. The gentleman, seeing no better opportunity, accepted of his services, but his thin shanks trembled visibly, and when, about half way to the boats, the native slipped, it brought a terrific scream from the frightened voyager.

As we were all burdened with our traveling equipments, each tried to take what they could. As a consequence many an article was dropped by its frightened owner and went bobbing over the smooth surface of the bay ; gripsacks, hand satchels, shawls, etc., were seen occasionally, floating on the waves ; they were, however, generally recovered by the agile natives. By the small boats we were conveyed to the ship's side, where a pair of steps were lowered to the water's edge, and by this means we ascended to the deck. If the sea happened to be rough, it was with great difficulty that the boats could keep their position near enough to the steps, in which event there was danger of losing one's footing and slipping between ; fortunately we had no serious accident. After the completion of the railroad across the Isthmus a staunch wharf was built by the company, and vessels since steam up to the wharf, receiving and delivering freight and passengers without the inconvenience which the early emigrant experienced. A gentleman whom I met years afterwards, and who had shortly before visited the East, remarked: "Well, the railroad is completed across the Isthmus; the passengers step off the ship on to the cars—all very nice and very

pleasant; but there's no more mule back ride, no more post back ride, and not a bit of fun."
After much hurry and toil our gallant ship was freighted and filled, and a strong breeze having sprung up, the sails were unfurled, and under steam and sail she swung round and rapidly put to sea. We glide past fragrant islands, rich with their wealth of verdure, their quaint homes nestling in orange and mango groves, the cattle and flocks of goats feeding on the hills—all seen indistinctly through the soft, filmy haze of the tropic seas. With the little boats idly resting in cove or on sandy beach, one recalls to memory the beautiful lines:

> "For they sail their ships
> Through the waters that slip
> Among the bright isles of the good and the blest."

Indeed it was difficult to associate a thought of other than "the good and the blest" with such a picture. One was fain to think that life might pass in such a place without a jarring note or sound of discord to mar the serenity of its luxurious beauty. But around on every hand were the evidences that ignorance and superstition and the despotism of Papal power held dominant sway. No free schools of enlightenment instructed them in progress and intelligence, and scarcely yet had the illuminating dawn of Christian civilization shed its first faint beams on this gifted tropical land.

Soon the green shore and the verdant islands were lost to view in the dim rim of the ocean. For days it was ours to see nothing but the blue expanse of waters, its myriad fish, and at rare intervals, a stray sea-bird. With what pleasure we sat at night at the prow of the vessel and watched the luminous phosphorescent light, which the ship ploughed up like myriad sparks of fire, as she skimmed through the dark blue water. Often a shoal of flying fish were blown across the vessel's deck; numbers were caught and examined; they were provided with fin-like wings, with which they were enabled to fly with the wind quite a distance. Large black fish were often seen, throwing jets of spray many feet in the air; these fish resemble whales. Porpoises, sharks, and the beautiful changeable dolphin, were at times seen. Early one morning we awoke to find that the mountainous coast of Mexico was plainly visible on our right, and were told that we were entering the harbor of Acapulco. The bay of Acapulco is perhaps one of the handsomest land-locked harbors in the world. Rock-ribbed and rock-bound, it is surrounded on all sides save the one point of entry. The gray dawn was just stealing over the sleeping water as the vessel cast anchor some distance from the shore. Of the town itself little could be seen; but the old fort, partly dismantled and dilapidated, but still occupied by the flower of Mexican chivalry, frowned grimly down from its commanding elevation. From the fort the beach sloped gently to the water. Out from the shore came numerous small boats, resembling canoes, impelled by natives and laden with the most delicious fruits of the tropics, and with rare sea-shells and other curiosities peculiar to the country. They drifted alongside the ship and in broken English offered their wares for sale. Up from the salt sea there floated the fragrant aroma of oranges, pineapples, bananas, lemons, etc., and a brisk trade in these articles commenced. Baskets, with long strings attached, for the purpose of drawing our purchases up to the deck, a distance of some 30 or 40 feet, were furnished by the natives. Twenty-five large oranges for 25 cents, pineapples 25 cents each, and everything else in proportion, and soon bunches of the beautiful fruit festooned every compartment of the vessel. The long saloon was as fragrant as a tropical garden; we had effectually dispelled for that voyage the peculiar salt water smell—the odor of pitch, paint, etc. Most of the passengers ate sparingly, though the tempting fruit looked delicious; but the dread of malaria—"Panama fever"—against whose fatal attacks all had been warned, kept their appetite in check.

Having sold out, most of the boats withdrew

and then the diving commenced. These Mexicans take to the water as naturally as a duck; they seem to be as much at home in the water as out of it. Boys, youths, and full grown men would plunge headlong from the prow of their boats in order to secure the small coins which the passengers, in infinite amusement, tossed from the vessel. Many a time the dusky figure of a Mexican disappeared far out of sight as he searched for the coin, but reappearing, he blew the water from his mouth and shook his shaggy hair like a dog, and was ready for another dive.

CHAPTER VI.

STORY OF THE CASTAWAYS — ON WATER ALLOWANCE — COMMITTED TO THE DEEP — LEFT TO PERISH.

Here in this rock-bound harbor was brought more vividly to my recollection, the story of my husband's early experience as first related to me. In the spring of 1852 he took passage from New Orleans by way of Central America for California. His ticket took him only as far as Aspinwall, where it was supposed that vessels would be in readiness at Panama to take them the remainder of the journey. That year there was a very heavy emigration by sea. To supply the demand, companies of speculators chartered old, unseaworthy vessels, and provisioning them on the cheapest plan, put to sea. In consequence, some of them were lost, and some were stranded on the Mexican coast, and the passengers abandoned to their fate. So great was the emigration that the port was crowded with eager emigrants waiting for vessels to take them on. After remaining in Panama some time, my husband, in company with a number of others, took passage on a sailing vessel which proved to be an old condemned hulk, refitted by a swindling company, and not even "good for this trip only." Before purchasing tickets, a number of the passengers applied to the American Consul at Panama for information in regard to the vessel, the company, etc., and were assured by him that the *Russell*, the name of the vessel on which they were to sail, was a seaworthy vessel, and that the company that fitted her out was perfectly reliable and responsible; they therefore purchased tickets, paying $160 to San Francisco. This sum in many instances was all the money many of the passengers could command. Soon after setting sail, they found to their dismay that the ship was poorly provisioned and meagerly supplied with water. To add to their anxiety, for days and days the wind ceased to blow, and they lay becalmed in the awful heat of the torrid sun, under the equator.

It was not long before they were put on water allowance. A half pint of dirty, thick liquid being a daily allowance. Their provisions consisted of hard, mouldy sea biscuits, rotten meat, mouldy rice, etc., none of it being eatable. Without nourishment, and suffering for want of pure water, it was not long before the Panama fever seized on the weakest and most delicate, and the measles in an aggravated form, also broke out among them. Many were prostrated and lingered for days and even weeks, piteously moaning in their delirium for home and absent friends, and at last died afar from those they loved; a slow death of disease and starvation, without a draught of pure water to moisten their dying lips. Among the number of that hopeful band, more than twenty died and were solemnly committed to the deep — their half-starved and wretched companions, helpless witnesses to the mournful truth. At last, after a period of 53 days, they neared the port of Acapulco. Here the captain anchored his vessel, and having abandoned it, left the passengers to whatever fate might have in store for them. Cast in a foreign port, without friends, and many of them without money—they realized the helplessness of their condition, and dark rumors were afloat of lynching the author of their miseries, but these rumors reaching the captain's ears, doubtless accelerated his departure, for he took passage on the next steamer bound for San Francisco. Those of the passengers who had money did so, also, but many had not a dollar, and were forced to remain. They applied to the American Consul at Acapulco, and to his shame be it said, he did nothing whatever to assist them in any way. Most of them were sick, all were weak and feeble from long starvation and lack of nourishment; they however obtained fresh water but could get nothing to eat without money. Without money and without friends, and unable to understand the language of the natives, they could do nothing—this handful of half-starved men, but to prolong existence as best they could, in the hope that sooner or later they would succeed in escaping on some passing vessel. Such was their almost hopeless condition.

The provisions which the ship still contained had dwindled down to mouldy rice and mouldy sea biscuits, the biscuits to all appearance having been baked years and years before, and were so hard as to effectually resist all efforts to break them, and when chopped open by means of axes or hatchets, they were full of green and yellow mould, and alive with small black bugs. The starving men often soaked these biscuits in the swill-barrel at the cook house—this being all that stood between them and starvation They were not however alone in their miseries and misfortunes. They found on their arrival that two or three vessels had preceded them, having been cast into port and abandoned by their captains. These vessels had been fitted out by the same company that fitted out the *Russell*. It was without doubt a preconceived arrangement to agree to take them through to San Francisco, exacting full fare, and then cast them ashore at Acapulco. The American Consul at Panama was suspected of being interested in the speculation. At least his conduct was reprehensible, as he had not taken the trouble to acquaint himself with the character of the vessels, but not the least shadow of an excuse could be found for the conduct of the Consul at Acapulco. Here were a number of his own countrymen starving and friendless—without the means of assistance, who had been cast ashore at the foreign port where he held his position. They applied to him for assistance, and he did nothing whatever to aid them.

Had it not been for hope, they could not have survived—the strongest constitution must have succumbed; but Hope, the blessed illusion, still beckoned them on—kept vigils by their emaciated forms in the gloom of midnight; held up her beacon light, brighter than the tropic sun; whispered sweet dreams in their waking and slumbering hours, and through want and sickness and delirium, still held out to their wondering visions the golden promises that had first lured them from home and friends. As days passed on, by degrees the little band was thinned; some died, and some were stowed away on other vessels. Six weeks of this monotonous time passed away. Ships often came, laden with their freight of passengers, and at last, one bright morning, when the fine steamer *S. S. Lewis*, with her humane captain, came into port, bound for San Francisco, my husband, despairing of receiving aid, determined to make a desperate effort to escape. In company with two or three others, he walked on board the vessel, immediately set to work among the sailors, and mingled with the crew. When fairly out to sea, he went to the Captain and plainly told his story, at the same time expressing his willingness to work for his passage. The Captain, a noble and humane man, replied: "Well, that's all right. I'll give you a good, easy job," and directed him to wash the decks once a day. It was better fortune than was anticipated. In those days so-called "stow-aways" were often disposed of without much ceremony. A large rock on the Mexican coast was pointed out to me, where it was said that an inhuman captain of a ship, on finding a "stow-away" on his vessel, had him conveyed and there left him to perish. The rock was above water in low tide, but was completely covered by the sea in high tide. When found on his vessel they were nearing this rock, and the tide being low, he had him taken in a boat and left there. Some kind natives happened to see his perilous situation and went to his rescue. The story, which doubtless was true, has invested the rock with imperishable fame. On arriving in San Francisco, my husband learned that the authorities there had heard of the forlorn and helpless condition of the passengers of the "Russell" and other vessels at Acapulco, and had sent a ship to their relief. What must have been their feelings of gratitude and thankfulness on their safe arrival after so long and perilous a voyage—a voyage which, from the time they left the port of New Orleans till they landed on the Pacific shore, occupied a period of nearly six months. To those who now make the journey from New York to San Francisco in six or eight days, these old stories of the early emigrants' journeys and voyages, fraught with peril, romantic adventures and hardships, seem like a sensational novel. For the most part, they are being rapidly forgotten. Now and then we see a gray-haired pioneer relating his early experiences; but the noble ranks of the early pioneers are growing sadly thin, and the young and rising generation is filling up the vacancies. When we look abroad upon the land, and see the wealth of her splendid cities, and the beauty and prosperity of her country homes, how little we think of the priceless treasures that were poured out for their purchase—of the toil and self-denial and sacrifice of those whose first footsteps left their impress on her soil.

CHAPTER VII.

A GRAVE BY THE SEASIDE—THE MEETING OF A STEAMER—THE SHIP ON FIRE—STANDING ON THE SHORE.

Before leaving the harbor of Acapulco, let me direct the reader's attention or memory to a grove of palm trees at the northern extremity of the bay; drooping and cool, the luxurious leaves seem trailing their slender points in the rippling water. In the bosom of the grove is the grave of a young American lady. The story is one full of touching interest, and was related to me by an eye witness of the occurrence. The captain of a ship was taking his young and beautiful sister to the Sandwich Islands for her health, but when within a short distance of Acapulco she died. Within this lonely grove of palms her grave was made.

And there they laid her, 'mid the dark, dim
Shades, where orange flowers ever bloom above her tomb;
Near the broad bay, sheltered from the ocean's storms,
Where tropic breezes softly blow; and voyagers upon
The sunlit sea look on her place of rest and heed
It not—unknowing that beneath those shadowy
Palms, in this secluded spot, a gentle maiden sleeps.

Though our short stay at the port of Acapulco was full of interest, and served to dispel for the time the monotony of the voyage; yet when the vessel swung round, and with her prow turned northward was steaming up the coast, we looked ahead with eager hopes, knowing that with no untoward circumstances, and with fair weather, in a few short days—

"That upward from yon sun-lined main
We soon should see the golden shore."

Up to this time little sickness and no deaths had occurred, but one morning we heard that a young German, with whom we were slightly acquainted, was very sick. He had eaten too much of the "forbidden fruit," fever ensued, and soon he was raving in delirium. His ravings, in broken English, were pitiful to hear. Nothing, however, could alleviate his sufferings; he lingered so for a few days, and one morning I woke to find that an ominous stillness reigned about his state-room—it was the awful silence of death. In the still watches of the night his spirit had passed away. A little band of friends gathered around and prepared his body for burial. A burial at sea is one of more than ordinary solemnity. The body was brought on deck and sewed securely in a canvas sheet, a weight being placed at the feet, and, while the steamer lay to and silently floated on the waves, friends and companions gathered around, and in the soft glow of the evening sunset a chapter was read and a prayer solemnly offered up. The remains were then placed on a board, feet outward, and amid the awful stillness it was slowly lowered into the bosom of the ocean— the waves parted, closed over the inanimate form, and all that was mortal of one who had lately moved among us, the picture of life and high health, had sunk to rest in that dreamless sleep that knows no awakening until "the sea shall give up its dead." To most of us he was a stranger, but doubtless in the far off Fatherland some loving heart broke over the sad news of his early death, and waiting hearts hoped anxiously for letters from the absent one—letters that never came, and how vainly they listened for the footstep and the sound of the familiar voice that was destined never again to wake the echoes of home. Three times afterwards we were witnesses of the solemn and mournful ceremony of a burial at sea.

Still steaming up the coast we saw, one bright

3*

day, far ahead of us, a faint object on the rim of the horizon; each moment it becomes more palpably real, and we are soon conscious that it is a vessel nearing us. How shall I describe the meeting of a steamer on the wild loneliness of the ocean? Dimly we see her masts and rigging, and her black hull ploughing through the dancing waves. All eyes are centered on the object; nearer she comes, over the deep, like a thing of life, sails and pennants and flags streaming in the breeze, and a dark vapor of smoke trailing like a cloudy veil to the windward; we hear the throb of her mighty engines, the dip and splash of her revolving wheels— nearer she comes! There's a jingling of little bells, a cessation of the throbbing of the engines, the paddle wheels are still, and gently gliding she floats upon the waves—a queen of the sea. Crowded on the prow are the passengers, waving hats and handkerchiefs, while cheer upon cheer rings like welcome music over the wild waves. The shouts are caught up on our side, and echoed back again and again. A small boat puts out from the steamer, manned by two jolly tars, and bearing the captain or first officer, who boards us and presents our captain with the latest news from California. There is an interchange of news, of friendly feeling, and soon we see the small boat returning. Again there is a jingling of the little bells, a heaving of the engines, and the wheels begin to revolve; a dip and a splash of the wheels, and then another cheer rings clear and musical, with echo upon echo, and the steamers have passed. How like the fleeting vision of many a winsome face we have met on the broad ocean of life! Though the event in itself seems trivial, yet the meeting of a vessel in mid ocean and a friendly interchange of salutes, is like a green spot in the wilderness, or like a friendly face in a foreign land. It breaks the monotony of thought; it breaks the monotony of the view of endless waves forever rolling outward toward the great sun, which seems to set within their depths.

We passed one fair day the dark and desolate looking Island of Marguerita. Its rocky headlands and inhospitable shores had a short time before been the scene of a terrible disaster. In 1853, the "Independence," bound for San Francisco, when near the island struck on a rock. The thrilling story of the wreck was related to me by a friend, who was one of her passengers. Soon after striking, it was discovered that the ship was on fire; every effort was made to quench the flames—crew and passengers worked bravely, and succeeded in keeping it in check until they neared the island. It was the captain's hope to drive her on the beach. A scene of the wildest confusion now ensued; as the ship was filling with water the boats were immediately lowered, but so eager were the excited passengers to escape, that the first two or three boats were overloaded, and amid the din and general confusion, and the terrified shrieks of men, women and children, they sank before they left the side of the ship. The excitement amounted to a panic. Hundreds of passengers jumped overboard in the vain hope of swimming to the shore. As they touched the water, they were grasped by those who were already drowning; others joined them, and clinging to each other in groups and knots in the struggle for life, and in the agony of despair and death, they sank to rise no more. It was useless to endeavor to swim when the sea around the vessel was full of drowning men.

An attempt was made to save some by means of a strong cable which was attached to the ship, a boat having succeeded in reaching the shore and securely fastening the other end. The rope was soon filled, but so great was the strain upon it that it broke midway, precipitating the passengers into the sea. My friend and his companion were expert swimmers, but the distance and the roughness of the sea rendered the attempt doubtful. Most of the women and children were saved; the captain stood with pistol in hand, declaring he would shoot down any man who tried to escape in the boats before the ladies were all saved. My friend and his companion were calm and self-possessed; they witnessed the terrible scene, and concluded to remain on board as long as possible, and when the vicinity around the burning vessel was cleared of the dead and drowning, they would make a brave attempt to swim for their lives. At last the auspicious moment arrived. The heat was now becoming intolerable, and the ship was rapidly sinking. Realizing their awful situation, they looked into each other's faces—"now for it," said one, and hastily divesting themselves of most of their clothing, they looked ahead, and seeing the way was clear, they simultaneously made a bold leap from the doomed ship. "We took it easy," said my friend, when relating the story, "resting occasionally, and then going ahead with even, steady strokes; but I found before proceeding half the distance, that fatigue was telling on me. I rested oftener, my companion always keeping near, but somewhat in advance. My limbs began to feel numb and torpid; a terrible weakness and lassitude was stealing over me, I looked and saw that the shore was slowly growing nearer—but every stroke now required my utmost strength, I looked again, and saw my companion standing on the shore and beckoning me, but my strength had failed—not even his cheers could renew my energy. It required all my efforts to bear myself up. Suddenly I felt myself borne onward by a strong wave, and with joy unspeakable, I realized that my hands touched the sands of the shore! With that thrill of rapture, all consciousness fled. When I awoke, I was resting 'high and dry' on the warm sands of the beach—out of the reach of the tide. By my side sat my companion, weak and faint, he too had had a close race for life; but reaching the shore some moments in advance of me, was just able to drag my senseless form out of the way of the receding waves." The scene was one which well might fill with dismay the stoutest heart. In the offing, tossed by the surging waves, was the dismantled ship, from stem to stern a complete mass of lurid flame. On the rock-bound beach, gathered in groups, were the pitiful remnant of destitute passengers. Some weeping bitterly and calling on those they loved, searched eagerly the bodies of the dead that the waves had cast up, in the hope of recognizing a friend. Most of the women were saved, but some of them had lost all that hitherto lent to life its brightest charm—a husband. brother or son, Of all that hopeful and happy throng that took passage on the staunch and noble ship, only a small remnant remained alive, and those were cast on a desolate island, half-clothed, without shelter, and nearly destitute—the outlook was indeed a gloomy one. A small store of provisions had been hastily thrown into one of the boats. But relief soon came; by some means, the news of the disaster soon reached San Francisco, and a ship was sent to their assistance. Whatever may have been said of the "greed of gold," which prompted thousands to seek California in its earliest days, it had no effect in closing their hearts to the cry of suffering. Their sensitive hearts responded quickly to the appeals of sorrow and misfortune, and with open-handed generosity they were ever ready to relieve the wants of the destitute and distressed. And be it said, too, to their honor, that the habit has not "grown weary in well doing." The many charitable institutions and homes for the friendless, stand as eloquent monuments to their noble deeds.

CHAPTER VIII.

THE QUEEN OF THE WEST—"THE HONEST MINER"—TOWARD THE MINES.

At the close of a long, fair day, the 26th of October, 1854, our voyage was nearing its completion. The sea was possessed of that happy quiet known to the Pacific. Over its bosom the myriad lights reflected and radiated from the gold of the vanished sun. The dancing waves seemed joyously luring us onward. To the right the rocky headlands of the coast of California became each instant more distinctly visible, and wrapt in the blue haze of distance and dimly seen in the gathering twilight, we discerned the gray wings of the Golden Gate, as though thrown open to receive us. A dreamy vapor, of soft, gray tint, wrapt its battlemented heights, between which flowed in ceaseless grandeur the broad surface of the sea. As night drew on, the myriad stars in the blue dome of heaven cast their clear reflections upon the water, and lit like beacon lights our pathway on the deep. With what happy hearts we neared the shore—the golden shore—the land of enchantment, of beauty, of dazzling wealth. Floating outward from the dusky rim of "the long, low-lying golden strand," came the sweet land breeze, so fragrant to our senses, so grateful to the weary voyager. With hearts elate and eyes happy with delight, we strain our vision to catch a glimpse through the dusky shadows of the night of the imperial city of the west— the queen of the Pacific! Out of the gloom there flashes a light! another, and yet another, and lo! before our enraptured vision, she sits enthroned upon her thousand hills, her myriad lights flashing and radiating like so many thousand gems far out on the bosom of the tranquil bay. To us the strange, bright land means *home*, and the steamer having moored at the wharf, we gratefully and with happy hearts take up our line of march for the shore. How awkwardly and unsteadily our "sea legs" navigate for a time the smooth and level wharf and plank walk. So long accustomed to the pitch and toss and careening motion of the ship, we with difficulty graduate our locomotion to the solid, unyielding surface of mother earth.

Well, reader, if you have ever been on ship board you will know with what pleasure—nay, unspeakable delight—we sat down to a supper of beefsteak, eggs, fresh butter, etc., and lingering over it all was the delicious fragrance of home and land, and we may be excused if with an unusual flow of spirits we next morning arose and looked out upon the broad, green land, and felt that we were free to roam wherever we list. No longer imprisoned in the narrow confines of the vessel, at the mercy of wind and wave, but standing on American soil and gazing over the broad and beautiful land, we felt that it was ours. Even at this early date San Francisco possessed many of the characteristics of a well developed city. For the most part the buildings were hastily erected wooden structures built to supply the immediate demand, but it contained many handsome and costly edifices, numerous churches, schools, public halls, and one fine theater. Situated as it was among the sand hills, the streets extended over hills and hollows, very little attention at that early date having been paid to grading and leveling. A large part of the business portion of the city was built over the bay—an insecure foundation one felt it to be, and which it proved in many instances; the rotting away of the planks on the sidewalks and wharves created the fatal "man traps" so well remembered of those early times, and which rendered it unsafe for pedestrians at night, especially strangers. The city of San Francisco was peculiar in many respects. When we come to reflect that only six years before it was an insignificant trading post, known as Yerba Buena (sweet herb), with no stir and none of the energetic activity that marks the thriving metropolis, and possessing only a few hundred inhabitants, we look upon its sudden growth and evidences of wealth as something akin to enchantment.

In one short year, the year of 1849, it increased in population from two to twenty thousand. We look in wonder upon its crowded wharves, with merchandise from every land; its thronging thoroughfares, filled with energetic citizens and strangers; and out upon the crescent rim of its beautiful bay, and see steamers, ships and vessels of every description and of every nationality, riding at anchor or arriving and departing. In wonder and admiration we ask: Whence comes this change? What magic has wrought this wonderful transformation? The mystery is solved in the answer: *Gold!* the powerful lever that moves the civilized world.

Since the first discovery of gold, at Sutter's Mill, near Coloma, in January, 1848, the auriferous metal had poured in almost ceaseless profusion into the city from the mines in the interior. One could hear its musical ring from day to day in the crowded business houses and banking establishments; and night and day the gambling saloons, fitted up in glittering splendor, held their gilded portals open to the professional sharper and the unskilled dupe. As San Francisco was the nucleus of all traffic on the Pacific Coast, the "honest miner," having "made his pile," returning homeward, spent a few days in the city; or, wishing to have a rest and a good time, came hither. Away from friends, and weary of the thronging masses that surged up and down the busy streets, lonely and homesick, the open and hospitable doors of the gambling saloons presented a pleasant temptation. Inside was light, cordiality, music, and around the long tables centred an unwonted attraction. Groups of men stood eagerly watching the players, as fortunes changed hands on a throw of the dice or the turn of a card. Under such circumstances, what wonder, if becoming mad with play and reckless with drink, men risked all, and losing, ended life by their own hands.

The peculiar characteristics of the society of this young and wondrous city were due to the very circumstances to which it owed its growth and onward march. The potent cry of gold, its discovery and profusion, had reached not only the Eastern States, but had spread over all parts of the world. Representatives of every quarter of the globe flocked to its golden shores. Every language under the sun was syllabled on her crowded streets. Every denomination of religion was respected and tolerated. Here stood, in unostentatious modesty, the Christian's house of worship, and by its side was the gaudy pagan temple—the joss house of the Chinaman—also the synagogue of the Jew. Each worshipped his own peculiar God in his own peculiar fashion. There was but one god to whom all devotees bowed in universal homage, irrespective of "race, age, color or previous condition," without regard to politics or place of birth, each heart poured out the rich libation of its homage to the god *gold*. Gold was the grand incentive—everywhere was the extravagant display of wealth. Ladies promenaded the streets attired in delicate-hued silks and satins; others not so gayly, but just as extravagantly dressed, appeared in rich and heavy velvets and satins, and flashing with jems set in the pure yellow gold of the country. The grand opportunities of this far western slope offered rare inducements to all classes of men, unsuccessful politicians, lawyers, and "gentlemen of leisure" who belong to that vast class who, like Micawber, are always looking for "something to turn up;" and men of the worst character—thieves, gamblers, desperadoes, etc. —mixed in the crowded thoroughfares. In such a peculiar society, it would seem that it would require ages and ages to transfer or remodel it into anything approaching harmony and order. Though gold was the grand incentive, yet there were not wanting good men, men of noble worth and sterling principles, who on more than one occasion when justice slumbered and right was crushed, and wrong. riot and outrage ran through the country, by their wisdom and concerted movement saved and restored society to tranquility and order. No small degree of praise is due, also, to the noble Christian women, who having left home and early friendships, came with their families to sojourn in this new land. It was due largely to their influence and exertions that churches flourished, Sunday schools were inaugurated, and many societies for the relief of the sick, friendless and distressed were organized. Those early pioneer women were the very "Mothers of Israel" to the young, disorganized and reckless state of society at that time.

Time could not be taken to remain long in San Francisco. Our future home was nestling among the aromatic hills of the Sierras—thither one bright morning we turned our faces, and once more we were on the broad and beautiful bay; we enter the noble Sacramento—in its primitive beauty it was a lovely stream—clear as crystal, abounding in salmon and other fish. Since the mining era its waters have become unlovely and muddy. Barges and scows flock its bosom, bearing grain, vegetables, and produce of all kinds to the Bay. Along the banks are numerous Indian villages. Here, "Lo, the poor Indian," spears salmon and dries them in the sun. The Digger Indian is a wretched, dirty, miserable creature, so far removed in his habits from humanity, as to scarcely be deserving of the name. So hideous do the older ones appear, that they are often frightful. It was a long time before I could accustom myself to look at them without a feeling of repugnance. The absence of all the noble traits with which Fennimore Cooper and like writers have invested the Indian character, in them is painfully conspicuous. They are small in stature, indolent, treacherous and cowardly, and like their more noble brethren are fast passing away. It is with surprise and pleasure that we note the many prosperous looking farms or "ranches" as they are termed in the far west, along the banks of the river. The rich bottom lands produced a wonderful growth of cereals and vegetables, which brought exorbitant prices in market. Glimpses of numerous river towns, among them Vallejo, Benicia, Sacramento, etc., lent to the country an Eastern aspect, and having reached Marysville at the junction of the Yuba and Feather Rivers, a pretty town of several thousand inhabitants and a stirring centre of trade for the broad plains and many mining vicinities, we took the stage for Nevada City—the place of our destination. Broad plains and rich bottom lands hitherto undisturbed by the plow, the domains of "Uncle Sam," lay invitingly open to the energies and industries of the tillers of the soil. It was a popular idea at that time that the plain land was worthless, except for. grazing purposes. A few years, however, changed that impression.

CHAPTER IX.

SCENES IN THE MINES — THE "LONG TOM" — THE ROCKER — THE CHINAMAN, ETC.

Some miles from Marysville, we came in sight of the first mining camp. Down near the bed of the river miners were at work; some shoveling, some digging, and others throwing dirt into an odd-looking contrivance for saving gold—the "Long Tom," an improvement on the "Rocker;" the Rocker being about the first rudely-constructed appliance for that purpose. Up to this time, the Rocker and the Long Tom were in popular use in the rich surface diggings along the beds of the rivers. Gold was then plentiful and easily saved by the simplest process. The miner toiled day in and day out, cheered by the reward of yellow gold; and at night dreaming of home and loved ones, the music of the Long Tom, mingled with the sweet voices heard in his dreams. At first sight, a miner's camp was not to the newly-arrived Easterner a very attractive spot, being very often a collection of rude cabins built of unhewed pine logs, with chimney of stone or rock in the gable end. Above towered the tall, motionless pines, through whose branches the gentle wind made mysterious and fascinating music —below, roared the yellow waters of the river, and in the background, the yellow hillsides were seamed and scarred—the rugged surface laid open, scraped and marred by the pick and shovel of the indomitable miner. As we approached that part of the road which lay along the banks of the Yuba, mining camps became more numerous, some very attractive and pretty villages enlivening the scene. Here the innovations of the Chinamen were observed. Already in the early history of California they were beginning to crowd white men to the wall. At first they worked mines that white men had deserted, but gradually in their own unobtrusive way, possessed themselves of some of the most valuable surface or placer mines. But they worked their mines on a far different principle from that of others. Others paid their laborers high wages, boarding them on the best the country afforded. The Chinamen brought bands of ignorant Coolies from China, who were in reality mere slaves, subject to his commands and entirely obedient to his authority; he fed them on the cheapest diet, rice and other cheap articles of food, shipped from his own country; the clothing, too, was brought ready-made from China; they slept in tents or cabins deserted by other miners, on bunks made of boards and sacks for bedding, and a sort of stool or box for a pillow. In this way the Chinaman spent none of his golden gains in the country, but steadily and persistently robbed the country of its golden treasure. He sucked the life-blood from her veins, laid open her rich arteries of treasure, and in unremitting toil gathered it up and shipped it to his own land. Though California was a free State, and Americans on their own soil were not permitted to bring and keep slaves to toil in the mines or any other vocation, yet the Chinaman was tolerated in carrying on a system of slavery, more obnoxious and more ruinous to American interests than was ever African slavery in the Southern States. Strange inconsistency of our Government! As time wore on, the more thoughtful awoke to a realization of the true state of affairs. Everywhere bands of these yellow-skinned foreigners were working like swarms of ants, crowding out white men from the best placer mines—wherever they could get a foothold, there they were. Shipload after shipload was landed in San Francisco—and dispersing, wound their sinuous persistent way to the mines. The voice of indignation rose in strong protest against them. Legislation was appealed to, taxes were imposed on all foreigners, and exacted of Chinaman. A second time taxes were levied on foreigners, Chinamen alone being affected by it. They were required to pay four dollars per month for working in the mines, but they knew no such thing as discouragement. Whenever possible, they evaded the tax collector. When he made his appearance at a village, a runner was sent to the next, and thence to the next, and soon, as if by magic, swarms of Chinamen laden with provisions, bundles, etc., were seen ambling from the villages seeking a hiding place in the foot-hills; there they remained a few days till they supposed the tax collector had passed, and gathering again in the mines, were soon established at work. Not infrequently impositions were practiced upon them by the miners, who viewed them with dislike and suspicion. During the dry season, the "honest miner," ever ready for an opportunity to earn a "few scads," would occasionally arm himself with a large ledger, and donning a coat and assuming a solemn and official air, repair to a Chinese camp to "collect taxes." On such unlooked-for calls, the Celestials were generally taken unawares, and generally obedient, and cowardly delivered up "the ready." If, however, they were disposed to dispute or evade the point, the muzzle of a revolver compelled compliance. Such raids were regarded by many of the miners as a good "joke," and were related with much satisfaction. Even at this period they were regarded with great detestation, and the universal sentiment was against them. It was the first mutterings of the storm — whose rumblings have since been heard along the distant years, and the fury of which have at different times risen and subsided—but which to the prophetic eye, we fear, has not yet culminated. "Overhead the clouds hang low and heavy, as though the storm is stayed but not spent."

Notwithstanding all that has been done to stop their further immigration, true to their character, they are quietly and persistently penetrating our borders, and in every way possible, evading the law. What is to be the end of all this? is the pertinent query; a question that has agitated the country since the first years after the discovery of gold, "China cheap labor" is encouraged by monopolies—railroad corporations, steamship companies and the organizations that profit by their labor; but it is the working classes who have keenly felt their demoralizing and distressing influence, the industrious and deserving, whom by their cheap labor they have crowded to the wall and impoverished. In those years they had not as they have of late, supplanted white labor in the different branches of mechanical pursuits—large manufacturing establishments, and also in the rural districts where they are employed in vineyards hop-yards, clearing land, and in other ways, not to mention them as having entirely monopolized the position of cooks, house-servants, gardeners, laundrymen, etc. *In every branch of industry, white labor has been crippled and paralyzed* in consequence of our inability to cope with the low rate of wages for which Chinamen are satisfied to work.

CHAPTER X.

THE DELECTABLE MOUNTAINS — THE TOWN OF GRASS VALLEY — AN IRASCIBLE MINER.

How delightful was my first view of the mountains, the delectable mountains! Rising from the low foot-hills, swell upon swell and crest upon crest, until dim and vague their snowy summits were merged in the pale blue of the far horizon, and as the coach wound its way among the hills, the aromatic odors of pine, fir and other species of evergreens came to us with a pleasing sense of newness; then, too, the sun shone with a new and fascinating brilliancy, throwing its golden shafts through the dark trees that stood in solemn grandeur along the wayside, or illuminating the depths of cool cañons where the river swept its flashing waters onward. Everything was new and strange, and for me possessed an indescribable charm. The active and energetic towns of Rough and Ready and Grass Valley, presented many attractive home pictures. Here, too, were churches and schools. Wherever families sojourned, churches and schools were found — we say sojourned, for very few, if any, in those days contemplated permanently settling in the country; some set the limit of their stay to two years, some to three, but very few to more than five. At the expiration of their self-imposed exile they confidently expected to have made their fortune, and return "home." But as time wore on, and in many instances "fickle fortune" eluded their grasp, they came to love the strange, new country, its salubrious climate, the pleasant mornings and cool, restful nights, and saw that the earth wherever watered yielded abundantly, they began to *make homes,* to plant orchards and vineyards, and with a shivering feeling they looked back to the sterile, barren winters and the sultry heat of the Eastern States, and found that they were wedded to the new home, its very customs, the freedom of its lovely hills and valleys. Many, however, suffered keenly the tortures of home-sickness in vain yearnings to see the loved ones of old; like Rachael weeping for her children, they "would not be comforted, because they were not." At the hotel in Grass Valley where we stopped for dinner, I fell into conversation with the pleasant landlady. I remarked on the beauty of the surrounding hills and lovely view before us. "Ah, yes," she replied, "it is all very beautiful, but," with a little sigh, "it is not like home." I then knew, by the far-away look so full of sadness, that her gentle heart was pining for the old home-life, the dear companions and well-beloved associations. Her grieving heart doubtless echoed the sentiment—

> " I'm lone and sad—and why not be?—
> Upon this foreign strand,
> For o'er the deep, unfathomed sea
> Sweet th ughts will ever visit thee
> My home—my native land!"

The town of Grass Valley was noted as the place where the first quartz mill was erected and successfully run. It was for a long time the home of —- Delano (more generally known as "Old Block"), a genial writer of early days, whose "Chips of the Old Block," containing humorous sketches of crossing the plains, life in the mines, etc., were universally read. Here also dwelt, for some time, the erratic Lola Montez.

It was about three o'clock in the afternoon that the coach, enveloped in a cloud of dust, drove up to the entrance of the Metropolitan, in Nevada City. Around the hotel, and postoffice adjacent, groups of rough-looking miners were assembled; the narrow and busy streets were crowded with a motley throng. Having sought our room and divested ourselves of our traveling wraps, we walked out on the verandah, anxious to get a glimpse of what was to be our home for an indefinite period. Like a strange bird set down on a foreign shore, amid new sights and new scenes, I looked around. The city itself nestled cosily among the hills, in a dip of the mountains, the business portion being compactly built. Scattered around on the adjacent hills, which environ the city proper, were residence houses, cosy cottages and cabins of the miners—portions of the city reaching outward, as if striving to stretch its wings beyond the narrow limits of its busy centre. Over the hills, in every direction, were evidences of the track of the miner. The earth was seamed and scarred with ground sluices and perforated with holes—deep holes—where old shafts for prospecting had been sunk. It looked as though demon claws had scooped and hollowed and mutilated the bosom of mother earth. Long trains of sluice boxes were seen, through which roared and rippled a stream of yellow, muddy water; by the side of them bands of miners stood, with their shovels leisurely shoveling in the gravelly soil which contained the precious metal. Nevada City, at the time of which I write, was the center of numerous rich placer mines, and was a flourishing and prosperous place of business—a very pretty mining town, located among the lower Sierras, with a genial, salubrious climate, warm and pleasant winters, with very little frost and snow; hardy vegetables grow and flourish the year round. Its citizens were energetic and enterprising, and if one may judge from the manner in which several have since distinguished themselves, were possessed of more than ordinary intellectual gifts. A. A. Sargent, who has since won Senatorial honors, was at this time an obscure and unpretentious lawyer, whose feet had not then commenced ascending the ladder of fame. William Stewart was also a young unknown lawyer; and I recall many other names of lesser importance who have sprung into honorable notoriety, having for their stepping stone the little mountain town—Nevada.

Soon after our arrival, many of my husband's old mining companions came to visit us. What was my surprise to see them all, without one exception, dressed in the recognized uniform of the mines—coarse boots, duck overalls and the universal gray flannel shirt—this being the style adopted by all honest citizens, merchants, officials, mechanics, miners and others. No one in those days possessed the temerity to initiate broadcloth and a "biled shirt" on ordinary occasions, unless it was the sporting class of men—gamblers, thieves, road agents, etc. A well-dressed man was looked upon with suspicion. If one of "the boys," as the miners were universally called, should so far forget himself as to don a "stovepipe" hat, he was the mark of special derision and practical

4*

jokes, and was not long permitted to enjoy his new possession. In some unguarded moment the hat was knocked off, and amid uproarious mirth, was set upon by half a dozen fun-loving fellows, and soon rendered an uncanny object, "a thing that was, but ne'er will be again." Notwithstanding the rough appearance of the miners, one soon learned that beneath their coarse exterior throbbed noble souls and principles of high integrity. So much has heretofore been written about the desperate and lawless class of adventurers who came to California in early times; but a short residence in the country made it apparent that there was also another class—the picked men of every nationality flocked hither to better their fortunes and in quest of adventure; men of fine minds and finished education, men of culture and brain. As elsewhere, one had only to "choose their company, not let their company choose them." One was apt to wonder, on first introduction into the mines, if these bronze-bearded, gray-shirted miners were the only type of society the country afforded; but on better acquaintance was surprised to find that many of them were gentlemen of culture and refinement and education, and possessed of a polish of manners which well might cause the envy of a Chesterfield. During the dry seasons, the coat was an article of dress universally ignored, and for a miner to sport an umbrella in the rainy season was a weakness not to be tolerated. But in the heavy rains, especially the first rains of the season, the regular miner would don his rubber suit, boots, coat and hat, and standing out in the dripping moistness, enjoy the situation. This was considered "the correct thing." There was no music so sweet to the miner's ears as the droning melody of the abundant rains; to him it sang: more gold! more gold! In many places they depended entirely on the winter rains to work their mines. At this time comparatively few women were found at the mines. In such well-settled towns as Nevada and Grass Valley, there were quite a number; but compared to the number of men, they were few. A new arrival was the subject of general comment, and a group of miners generally assembled at "stage time" eager to get "news from home," and I may add, to catch a glimpse of the newly arrived lady passengers. If somebody's wife, or somebody's sister had come, the first questions propounded were — "Is she pretty?" and then, "Is she young?" The eagerness with which men sought to catch a glimpse of a "new lady's" face, was remarkable, and to the lady, extremely embarrassing. It was not the rude stare of impertinence or insolence, for excepting perhaps the one thing, gold, the honest miner had more genuine reverence for a *true woman*, than anything earthly. The deferential courtesy which emanated from the heart, and was not a mere formality, was due to circumstances. An article is valued according to its scarcity. The courtesy and reverence accorded to women in those early days, was a marked feature of society in the mines. A little anecdote will serve as illustration. Years after, when residing in one of the interior valleys, I became acquainted with a lady whose girlhood had been spent in the mining town of E. In conversation with her one day, she referred to the old chivalrous politeness which marked that era and place, and with some enthusiasm exclaimed, "Why, when I resided in E., I never walked up street without having *forty hats* lifted to me as I passed! but Mrs. S., it is the God's truth that I haven't had a hat lifted to me since I have lived in this village." The scarcity of women, and the corresponding appreciation in which they were held, was one of the peculiar features of the society in the mines. Entering a lecture room, concert or theatre, the house would be crowded with men, with perhaps half a dozen ladies occupying the front seats. Balls, evening parties and socials, though of frequent occurrence, often proved a "delusion and a snare," to a large majority of the masculine portion. If the presence of half a dozen ladies supplemented by three or four little girls, ranging in age from four to ten years could be obtained, a grand ball was in order. The hall was filled with gentlemen; twenty to one lady, being a fair average; engagements were entered into so far ahead, that unless a lady frequently referred to her memoranda, she was liable to make a mistake. If so, some gentleman would be slighted, somebody's feelings wounded, words followed, a little unpleasantness ensued—the lady's particular friend would take it up, and about this time the floor manager appeared on the scene, and escorted the now highly enraged gentlemen from the hall, where the matter was generally settled outside in a manner most satisfactory to the parties.

In consequence of the scarcity of families, "keeping bach" was the prevailing style of living among the miners. From four to six men usually "cabined" together, taking turns doing the cooking week about. A very humorous story was told us of a very irascible miner, which will illustrate some of the annoyances and grievances to which they were subject. At Wood's Ravine, some four miles from Nevada, in a certain cabin, three mining companions were "keeping bach" together. Not to be too personal, we shall designate them as A, B and C. One Monday morning, B arose early, it being "his week" to cook, kindled the fire in the huge fire place, and filling a sheet iron camp kettle with water, into which he put some potatoes to boil, swung it over the fire, and began preparations to make some biscuits. A few moments later he noticed that the fire was out and there was no water in the kettle; rekindling the fire and filling the kettle, he resumed his bread making; some time elapsed, and having occasion to look at the fire, he was astonished to see that there was not a spark, and on inspection found that the kettle was again dry. This time muttering a "bad word," and refilling the kettle and starting the fire anew, he continued making the bread. Becoming absorbed in that scientific occupation, he forgot all about the fire; but on going to put the bread into the "Dutch oven," he was brought to a halt, by observing that instead of a glowing fire, there was nothing but black embers; the kettle, too, was dry. This was "too much"—at least for B's explosive nature. Jerking the kettle from the rack, and giving vent to a series of exclamations, he emptied it of its contents, and holding it up to the light, saw with indignation and disgust, that there was a large hole in the bottom! Striding to the door he opened it, threw the kettle on the ground and began jumping on it, then seizing an ax near by, he placed the kettle on a stump, and was mauling it with all his strength, accompanying each blow with remarks that were more expressive than elegant. The noise had long before awakened " the boys,' and one of them, C, an unpardonable wag, arose, strode to the door, and opening it, looked out at the irate B, and coolly remarked, "Give it to it, Bill, give it thunder!"

What sacrifices men suffered—what discomforts they endured—what untold yearnings for home and loved ones! What exile and isolation did they not experience for *gold!* How meagerly at the last were they (the vast throng) requited. Only the voiceless mountains, scarred and seamed with their ambitious endeavors, stand mute monuments of many a story of wreck and disappointment.

CHAPTER XI.

THE VIGILANCE COMMITTEE — DESTRUCTION OF NEVADA CITY BY FIRE — SNOW SLIDES IN THE MOUNTAINS.

In consequence of the lax manner in which justice was administered during the first years of the country's history, it may not inaptly be called the age of crime. Nowhere was life and property safe. The daring exploits of noted highwaymen, murderers, thieves and robbers of every description, and the swindling operations of depraved politicians are familiar to the readers. It was at this time, while residing in Nevada City in 1855-56, that the whole country was aroused to indignation by the murder of a peaceful citizen of San Francisco—an honorable and brave man, James King of William, a journalist, who had dared to speak out openly in defence of the right. For this he was shot in open day in a public part of the city. The news spread over the country like wild-fire, and knowing well the leniency of the law, and the depravity of public officials, the people took the law in their own hands, and reorganized the "Vigilance Committee," which had disbanded in 1851. The murderer of King was speedily hung, a few other executions occurred, and Judge Lynch for a time held supreme sway.

From this time dates the gradual dawning of better things in the moral atmosphere of the country.

In the summer of 1856, in July, the beautiful and flourishing mountain city of Nevada, was destroyed by fire. It was one of those calm, autumn-tinted days when the sun shone as it shines only in the heat of mid-summer, not a drop of water had fallen for months. Sitting at my window, my attention was arrested by a shout, and as I stepped to the door, out from the heart of the city there arose as if from hundreds of brazen throats, the cry of fire ! fire !! fire !!! along with the cry I observed a dense mass of black smoke curling upward, mingled with red tongues of fiery flame. With the exception of some fifteen or twenty staunch and handsome brick buildings, the city was built like all other mining towns, of fragile frame buildings—cloth-lined, and most of them cloth-ceiled and partitioned. Against the devouring element these offered no resistance. Families in the vicinity where the fire originated, had barely time to escape with their lives; those farther on, moved their goods out on to the streets, and as the flames advanced, still farther. Soon that portion of the town was swept clean of every building, and now the flames were spreading to Main street, in the vicinity of the brick buildings which it was hoped would afford some check to the advance of the rapacious monster. Vain hope! One after another, after a slight resistance, was seen to succumb to the devouring element and the intense heat. Around the staunch brick buidings the red tongues of flame circled and roared like the howling of demons, and yielding to their invincible fury, the fire burst from windows and roof, and the tottering walls fell. Ere long, the business part of town was a sea of flame! Not a vestige of a building remained, save one—one building alone stood the awful avalanche of fire — blackened and smoked and begrimed it stood alone, the only building left intact and erect on the spot of desolation and ruin. Though many long years have passed since then, the event is one that by me a mere eye witness will never be forgotten. The surrounding hills and suburbs beyond the reach of the flames were covered by the escaping inhabitants — women with their children seeking refuge from the fire, and strong men, some weeping over the loss of goods and worldly effects; most of them were burdened with all they could carry, some were hatless and coatless, and begrimed with dust and smoke in their futile endeavors to quench the flames. Many had lost all their worldly possessions, with nothing left but the clothing they wore, others saved their money and jewelry.

But the saddest chapter in this story of ruin

and desolation, was not yet revealed. After it was all over, and friend inquired for friend, it was ascertained that a number of persons had perished. It was supposed that many of the staunch brick buildings were "fire-proof," and acting on this belief, and in the mad excitement of the moment, several young men were known to have entered these buildings in the expectation that they could survive the awful deluge of fire. Vain delusion! Their bones were found in the cellars, whither they had fled in the suffocating heat. Some were identified by their watches and portions of clothing nearest the ground. So perished, in a mad freak of excitement and cruel delusion, some of the finest and most promising young men of the city. Time has obliterated in my memory their names and particulars of their sad fate, but doubtless this reference will reach the eye of some who have cause to remember sorrowfully the minute details.

The smoke had not cleared away from the ruins of the city, before numerous white canvas tents rose all over the blackened site, and as speedily as possible, the bones and remains of the unfortunates were collected and given burial. Scarcely had the flames subsided, before preparations for building were commenced. Teams were busy hauling lumber, and soon the hammer and saw were heard in every part of the burned town. Relief for the destitute and distressed was sent from mining camps and valley towns far and near, with the promptness and generosity so characteristic of the times. In the course of a few weeks Nevada emerged from her awful baptism of fire, rebuilt and renewed, many of her buildings being replaced by more substantial and finer ones than those preceding. Almost every mining town of any importance suffered from the effects of fire, in consequence of the fragile and inflammable character of the buildings, and in some cases the carelessness of the inhabitants.

Such was the delightful climate of the lower Sierras that it was a most pleasant place to make homes. Possessing a rich, fertile soil peculiarly adapted to the growth of fruit, vines and vegetables, it was no surprise that in a short time the numerous inviting sites for farms or ranches were located; and traveling among the mountains it was no uncommon thing even in those days to come upon a quiet farm nestling among the hills. A good "ranch" was more valuable than an ordinary gold mine. Farm produce of all kinds had a ready market in the towns and camps near by, and fruit, butter and eggs brought fabulous prices.

But mountain farming was not without its objectionable features. All land being mineral land, according to mining laws, if a gold bed was discovered on a ranch, the discoverer had the right, by paying for property destroyed, to open up his mine and sluice it all away. I have seen many beautiful farms undermined and sluiced away, and where once was a cosy home, surrounded by orchard, vineyard, grain-field, garden, etc., nothing remained but a "howling desolation." The insecurity of property in the mines prevented many from seeking to settle permanently there.

In the autumn of 1856, in harmony with the spirit of unrest then prevailing, we listened to to the voice of the siren, who whispered more gold ahead! ahead! and selling our comfortable home for half its cost, and disposing of our mines at a sacrifice, we moved to Chipps Flat, Sierra Co., in the upper Sierras, in the deep snow belt. Here we purchased several interests in a mining ditch—a ditch for the purpose of conveying water to the mines. The property was valuable and the mines flourishing, and settling here, we felt that we had invested in something that was certain and would bring in a handsome income soon. How vain are human expectations!

The little hamlet of Chipps Flat was situated in the heart of a rich mining district, above the deep cañon of the Yuba river. The latter part of the journey was made on mule back. The steep, winding, zigzag trails led down the cañon and up again, on the ragged edge of perilous precipices and over bare ledges of rock, up and still up, till the river looked from our towering eirie like a silver skein flowing in the dark chasm below. A single misstep and we were in danger of being hurled hundreds of feet. From one point towering far above the little hamlet we looked over the grand amphitheatre of mountains, rolled back as far as eye could reach, and remotely in the distance the gray swell of the vast plains bounded by the dim outlines of the Coast Range. Through the valley, distinctly visible, winds the sparkling Sacramento. On dusky nights in this clear atmosphere, the lights on the river steamers could be plainly discerned. From this towering point one counted no less than ten mining towns in the vicinity. Orleans, Moores and Woolseys Flat, Minnesota, Centerville, Alleghaneytown, Smiths Flat, Oak Flat, Lafayette Hill, and Chipps Flat; all more or less prosperous mining camps.

Many tons of rich ore were shipped from these localities. Quartz mining and "tunneling" were the principal features of industry, the busy stamping of the mills was a familiar sound. There one enjoyed all the advantages of the "beautiful snow;" it fell almost incessantly during the winter. It attained a depth of seven feet in the winter of 1856-57.

Avalanches or snow slides were of frequent occurrence, often resulting seriously to life and property. On one occasion my husband and a companion were at work on a "flume" several miles from home. The snow had fallen to a great depth and hung in masses on the side of the mountain. Their attention was arrested by hearing a roaring noise, and looking up, they saw an immense body of snow from the height above descending. For my husband to spring into the flume and lie down, was but the work of a moment; and after the avalanche had passed, he looked around for his companion. For some time he was nowhere to be seen—the huge body of snow had lodged in the bottom of the cañon some three hundred feet below; following this with his eye, and closely scanning every object, he at last saw a human figure sitting at the bottom of the cañon and surrounded by masses of snow. To his repeated shouts there was a faint wave of the hand. As speedily as possible, he hurried to him and found him bruised and bleeding and jammed on the rocks and brush over which he had been so rapidly carried. Fortunately no bones were broken, and after a short time an effort was made to reach home. Faint and weak, his companion was scarcely able to walk on level ground, but with help, and by dint of shoveling a pathway for a few steps and resting at intervals, they were at last enabled to reach the bank of the ditch where a road was partially broken. It was a long, weary and painful march, and after what seemed to be an interminable length of time, they reached the village.

Another serious cause of accidents in these heavily timbered mountains, was the rolling of huge timbers from the mountain tops. Large trees were often felled on the mountain sides, their limbs used for fuel and their ponderous trunks "staked up" and left to rot. As time went on, the stakes rolled away, and having slipped its fastenings, the tree, agreeable to the law of gravitation, descended, and woe to the humble cabin that stood in its way. I knew a lady who was one day standing in her house when all at once she was conscious of a grating, rumbling sound; before she had time to speculate as to its cause, there was a terrific shock, and immediately the whole end of the cabin was burst in, and the ponderous body of a tree stopped in the centre of the wreck. She was left on one side of the kitchen, surrounded by mutilated furniture and broken crockery, while the huge body of an ancient pine some six feet in diameter disputed her exit. In a neighboring town I saw at one time the ruins of three cabins that were leveled to the ground by the rolling of a giant of the forest from the heights above. A man and his wife occupied one of the cabins

—the lady was instantly killed, and her husband badly injured. In one of the other cabins a "lone miner" was sleeping, who escaped more fortunately. By some means he was thrown to the ground, face downwards. As it was a *ground floor*, he had a snug squeeze, but escaped unhurt, leaving the cast of his features in the yielding clay.

Such were some of the peculiarities of the higher Sierras. Early one fine morning in July, I found myself with a party of friends en route for that gem of the mountain —Sierra Valley, distant about 35 miles. As the journey had to be made on horseback, we had secured an early start. It was a grand and glorious ride! Thirty-five miles in one day on horseback over the winding trails of the Sierras! Now speeding through sweet, green vales, where the native grasses stand breast high to our horses, and crossing crystal streams and shadowy rivulets—climbing abrupt and rocky ascents, and anon, traversing the bald peak of some towering height, over beds of everlasting snow, where the force of the sun is powerless to melt its solid crystal. Far up in these elevated solitudes, miles and miles from any human habitation, we observed a lone mound, and turning aside, halted a moment. It was a solitary grave. There was no name on the mute head-board, and nothing to furnish a clue to the sad story; but time and neglect and the fury of the elements had not obliterated this lone, sad trace of the last resting place of a fellow being. "Lost in the snow," perhaps, we mused; a not uncommon fate which befel many a luckless gold hunter.

> No marble rears its stately head
>   To deck thy lonely pillow,
> No proud fame mocks thy humble bed—
>   Nor rose, nor weeping willow;
> But may the sigh by strange lips borne,
> Be wafted to thy spirit home.
>
> The wild winds played thy dying note—
>   The night frowned darkly on thee—
> Cold was the snow, thy funeral robe,
>   And stern the blast before thee;
> The night is past, the wind is still,
> Rest, pilgrim, on this storm-beat hill.
>
> Thou'lt hear no more the cruel blast
>   That Destiny threw round thee;
> For Death's dark wing has o'er thee past,
>   And stern's the Fate that bound thee,
> And stillness wraps thy silent tomb—
> Where mountain flowers about thee bloom.
>
> But may the sigh low breathed by her,
>   As sad she gazed above thee,
> Ascend into thy radiant sphere;
>   For those the friends who loved thee,
> For all must share a lonely grave,
> 'Neath deep oblivion's changeless wave.

The dusky shadows of twilight were fast gathering over the scene as we commenced the descent of the mountain that overlooked Sierra Valley. Green and beautiful it lay, surrounded on all sides by towering mountains; crystal streams flowed through its length, and herds of cattle fed on the luxuriant grass. Here we formed the acquaintance of "Alice," Mrs. Ordelle C. Howk, a warm-hearted and hospitable lady, and a writer of those early times, who contributed stories, sketches, etc., to "Hutching's Magazine" and other periodicals. She and her husband, with a few other families, comprised the few settlers of this romantic and sequestered vale. After spending a week in recreation and rest, we returned home.

CHAPTER XII.

A CHANGE OF SCENE — THE "WASHOE" EXCITEMENT — THE FESTIVE GRASSHOPPER — THE EARLY SETTLER.

After a few year's residence among the higher Sierras, we became weary of the deep snows of winter, the isolation of the locality, etc., and in December of '58, turned our faces valleyward, with the intention of farming. A few miles from Marysville we found a suitable location. The rich river bottoms of the Yuba that had not then been inundated by the despoiler "Slickens," yielded bountiful returns for the toil of the husbandman. All along the river were fine farms, with orchards, vineyards and grain fields. Many acres of the best land had not as yet been touched by a plow. And plain lands that could not be irrigated, at that day, were not generally thought worth farming.

Among the most noted orchards was Briggs', three miles from Marysville, a large and flourishing one. Fruit sold on the ground at 12½ cents per pound, yielding a handsome income yearly. Alas! how has the scene changed. Over all that smiling and prosperous region — over every foot of that rich alluvial soil — over orchards and vineyards, and prosperous farms, the dreaded "Slickens" has spread devastation and ruin. Where once was beauty and wealth and sweet homes, nothing remains but desolation—everything except the roofs of houses and the tops of trees buried in the slimy insinuating yellow debris. The introduction of hydraulic mining brought disaster and ruin to much of the richest and best lands of the State by flooding them with the yellow washings from the mines.

Up to 1859, very little attempt had been made to raise corn in the State—many entertaining the opinion that the soil and climate were unsuited for its production, but our corn crop that year on bottom land averaged one hundred bushels to the acre. In September of the same year, we attended the County Fair at Marysville, held in the old pavilion and grounds. It was a grand success; every branch of industry being represented, and the products of the soil were an interesting feature. It was not wanting in evidences of culture and refinement, and an interest in the arts and sciences to prove the wonderful and rapid march of progress and improvement in a young State not yet having finished her first decade.

The Fair was rendered memorable by the presence of one of the most noted men of the period — the great and lamented journalist, Horace Greeley. He had arrived in California a few weeks previous, having made that summer his celebrated overland journey by way of Ben Holliday's stage line.

What a deafening tumult of applause greeted him as he arose, a plain, farmer-like looking man—and made a speech entirely in harmony with his appearance.

The same year was marked by an event which cast a gloom over the entire State— the political duel which was fought by Judge Terry and the Hon. David C. Broderick, in which the latter was killed. The affair created great excitement and much comment; and as a remarkable event has taken its place in history. The feelings of the country which were aroused over the affair, are still fresh in the memories of those who were residents here at that time.

Towards the close of '59 the discovery of the Washoe gold and silver mines created wild excitement. Nevada, previous to its admission as a State, was known as the "Washoe" country. In keeping with the spirit of adventure, my husband, being an experienced miner, determined to form one of a party bound for the new gold region. I therefore concluded to visit during his absence my old home in the East; and early in 1860 I took passage with my two children on the steamship *Sonora* for New York, to remain as I then contemplated, a few months, or a year at most—but how little we know of the hidden mysteries of the future! How little I dreamed that nine long years, with their singular changes would pass ere I should set foot on the land to whose genial climate and many fascinations I was strongly wedded! But such are life's vicissitudes. Up to this time the first ominous whisperings of Civil War had scarcely awakened a serious sentiment on the far-off Pacific Coast; but I found on my arrival in the Eastern States that the threatening news of the on-coming storm pervaded every heart, and in April of the following year the bugle sounded the " Call to arms."

After the long and eventful journey I reached at last the familiar scenes of my early years, and once more on board of one of those grand and superb floating palaces of the Western waters, we were steaming down the queen of rivers, the beautiful Ohio. How familiar and yet how strangely altered seem the old landmarks! Her banks are gemmed with stately cities, rich in beauty and wealth, with towns and hamlets, with broad plantations and magnificent residences — the low-lying lands are now and then broken by rugged bluffs and picturesque and romantic scenery. They seem to glide past us like the vision's scene in dreamland. Steamboating on the western rivers in one of those old-time magnificent steamers was a mode of traveling that for comfort and supreme enjoyment is unsurpassed; but like many another custom of "Auld Lang Syne," has been superseded by more modern changes. How pleasant to pace slowly up and down the "hurricane deck" on quiet evenings when the sunset rays are gilding the tops of the noble trees that droop over the river banks! And not less charming is it to hear on the morning air, sang out in ringing tones, "Wood yard! wood yard!" Snatching a shawl if the air is cool, we select a seat on the "guards," and while the steamer is gracefully and grandly "rounding to," we have ample time to note the scene. Vast piles of cord wood flank the banks, and a woodman's cottage, low-browed and brown, is seen at a distance. Now the boat has touched the bank; a daring deck-hand springs ashore, and, with cable in hand, fastens it securely; the gang plank is shoved out, and the crew in long array file out to the wood yard; and, while they shoulder their burden and bear it on board, we listen and catch the familiar negro chorus, sung in their peculiar melodious intonation. There is brisk work for a few moments, the melodious music of mellow voices mingling with the clatter attending the "wooding up." Then we hear the mate's voice, in stern command, "Let go the cable! Haul in the plank!" Then there's a jingling of little bells—a puff of steam, the last man springs on board and we have soon left the wood yard far behind.

After lingering in the Middle and Western States for several months, I at last proceed on my journey, my final destination being the frontier country of Nebraska, then a Territory in the first stages of its settlement. Here my mother's family had immigrated during my six years' sojourn in California. Scarcely had I reached my journey's end before the bugle notes of civil war sounded from Fort Sumter, and the "call to arms" thrilled every heart, and here, as elsewhere, all was excitement, commotion and activity—companies were being drilled and regiments organized in all the "pomp and circumstance of war."

The frontier countries, though far removed from the seat of war and the vicinity of hostilities, suffered no little in consequence; the hard times caused by the war being felt more acutely on the border, for various reasons, than in the Middle and Eastern States. All articles imported to the country commanded exorbitant prices, while there was scarcely a market for home produce. The means of transportation were meagre and limited. Railroad facilities to the remote frontier, were scarcely dreamed of. During war times many articles reached fabulous prices. For illustration: Tea was four dollars per pound, coffee seventy-five cents per pound, calico fifty cents per yard, and muslin seventy cents per yard, and all imported articles in proportion; and though the country produced abundantly, the low price paid for home products made very distressing times. Corn, which was the staple, was ten and fifteen cents per bushel, butter eight cents per pound, eggs five cents per dozen. Add to this the fact that Indian depredations and hostilities continually threatened the remote settlements, and we have a not very attractive picture of the frontier during the years of the war. The country, in itself, was a rich and promising land, whose broad, rolling prairies and rich bottom land, free to the adventurous settler, offered fine inducements to those seeking homes on Uncle Sam's dominions.

My mother's farm, situated on the Nemaha River, was well out towards the confines of civilization, and "forty miles from any town." On more than one well-remembered occasion the cry of "Indians are coming" was wafted to us from the border, and packing our household goods in a wagon, and driving our stock before us, we turned our backs on the approaching foe, and making forced marches, sought safety in a more dense settlement. Here we consolidated our forces, and having sent out a scout to ascertain, if possible, the cause of the rumor, awaited the turn of events. The reports, at one time, at least, proved to be but too well founded. Two men of our acquaintance, settlers, several miles back, had been treacherously murdered at a station on the "big road," cattle had been stolen, and other depredations committed. The information that we received was to the effect that these two men, Messrs. Kelley and Butler were traveling, and had stopped at a station, and while there were warned by a friendly Indian that a band of Indians were about to attack them. It was not long before they made their appearance, and Kelley, unarmed, boldly advanced to meet them, extending his hand in token of friendship. The Indian immediately leveled his rifle, the bullet taking effect in Kelley's breast, who staggered to the house, sat down, and soon expired. The other Indians ran up and shot Butler, who, climbing to the loft, laid down and there died. In consequence of this outrage many settlers left their homes, their growing crops, and everything except a few portable articles, and fled in terror from the border, some never to return. Most of them, however, returned after a time, not without a feeling of insecurity, lest at any time the murderous savages would rise *en masse*, and massacre the few defenseless settlers scattered at intervals along the banks of streams, miles and miles from where relief could be obtained.

Though bands of roving Indians often passed through our neighborhood, no serious outbreak occurred, and when the war was over and peace declared soldiers were again garrisoned on the frontier to protect settlers and travelers, and once more a feeling of security prevailed. Immigrants came pouring in, and soon the dawning of the railroad era accelerated the march of civilization. Other causes of minor importance also operated against the immigrant of "ye early period," among them being notably the festive grasshopper. For years and years they came regularly, swarming down upon the luxuriant crops like an "army with banners." Unheralded and uninvited they came, in swarms so dense as in some instances to obscure the sunlight. If the careful husbandman did not immediately begin storing his crops there would soon be nothing left but the bare ground to tell where but a few hours before had been fields of waving corn, golden wheat, vegetables, fruit, etc. There was nothing that the rapacity of his nature would not devour—onions, garlic, tobacco—and having annihilated the tobacco crop, they sat in swarms on the fences and defiantly spit the tobacco juice in the faces of the ravaged farmers.

Before leaving this subject, I may be pardoned for referring to some of the peculiar features and incidents which belong essentially to those early times. The country being sparsely timbered, lumber as a consequence was scarce, and out on the frontier particularly so, and frequently settlers of limited means built in lieu of a house "a dug-out." In connection with this style of habitation an itinerant Methodist minister met with a ludicrous adventure. In traveling in a sparsely settled part of the country he lost his bearings, and wandered around for some time. At length night came on, black and moonless. After a long time he came to the bank of a stream, and knew if he followed it he would sooner or later reach a settlement. With this hope he began hallooing at intervals, but could find no habitation. After awhile he came to a field of corn and a well-defined road that led to a garden. Soon he heard the barking of dogs, but no house was visible. Weary and hungry and almost in despair, he mounted an eminence near by and gave vent to a shrill "halloo." Scarcely had the sound of his voice died away before there bounded up at his very feet the figure of a man, shock-headed and half-clothed, who inquired in dismay, "What on earth is the matter?" "Why, hulloo, where do you live?" said the traveler. "Why, I live at home down here. "Where do you live, and what do you want, and who are you?" "B'gosh I thought I was surrounded by a band of injuns." Explanations followed, and when "the settler" found that he merely had an inopportune call from a traveling divine he opened the door of his subterranean dwelling and hospitably entertained him. In relating it, the minister naively remarked: "I supose in my wanderings that night, I walked over several large and flourishing settlements."

More than a passing reference is due to the early settler of the border States, who belongs to that hardy and adventurous class that hew the road for civilization. With his worldly effects in a rickety wagon, covered with a bed-quilt and drawn by a pair of oxen, and with a small drove of cattle following, driven by a boy on a thin-legged pony, he with his family and little cavalcade penetrated the heart of the wilderness, and staking off a claim in this raw world, prepared to "make improvements;" that is, to build a cabin and break a corn-patch. One cannot contemplate his character without feeling for it the most profound admiration and respect. It was his to bare his valiant breast in the very van of advancing civilization; through his tattered rags the lonesome blizzards of the unpeopled prairies swept with reckless energy. His unshod and barnacled feet were exposed alike to the nipping frosts of early spring and the burning trails of summer saunterings, and upon his superanuated coonskin cap the merciless elements descended. He had come to the country in the dawn of adversity, and, having spent the best years of his manhood, was growing old and gray under the snows of many winters, and warped and bent by "hard times" and summer suns, and when I saw him last was still lingering on the "ragged edge" of hope—longing for the tardy van of civilization to cast its wave of better fortune at his feet.

The prevailing mode employed by the average writer in describing the early settler and the pioneer is to invest him with a character ignorant, uncultured and boorish; something after the following style : "Stopping in front of a rude, log hut, we uttered a shrill halloo! At the sound of our voice a tall, gaunt, lantern-jawed individual made his appearance and, with mouth open, viewed us with evident curiosity. In answer to our 'good day,' he said : 'Wall, stranger. How d'y'e do? Won't ye light?' 'No, thank you. Can you tell me if I am on the right road to B.?' 'Sartain, stranger, sartain. You jest keep right straight ahead, an' you'll *git thar.*'" Such is merely an overdrawn and exaggerated picture, for one is often surprised to find in these far frontier settlements the smallest and humblest abode being the homes of the educated, the refined and cultured, and almost invariably men of *vim*, enterprise and daring. In this instance they had immigrated here years before, and anticipated securing homes and advancing and prospering with the growth and development of the country, but the long years of the Civil War and local causes had lain a paralyzing hand for the time being on progress and improvement. Since the removal of these causes what a picture is here presented! Through all that country that was then an unsettled wilderness—the haunt of the hungry wolf, the cayote, the elk, antelope and buffalo—where still were seen the scattered remnants of the wigwam of the lone Indian, there have risen on their hunting-grounds and battle-grounds flourishing towns and pleasant villages. A network of railways cross and intersect each other, and along their route and on the vast prairies are fields of corn and wheat and comfortable farm houses, and verily, here has the "March of Empire" left the imprint of its shining footsteps!

CHAPTER XIII.

TO COLORADO — ACROSS THE PLAINS — FORT COTTONWOOD — ATTACKED BY INDIANS — A WATER SPOUT, OR CLOUD BURST — PIKE'S AND LONG'S PEAKS.

To those who had spent years in the genial climate of California, the rigorous winters, with their continuous snow-storms, and the tardy springs of Nebraska was a serious objection, and as my husband had returned to the East, we, with an unconquerable desire to dwell again in the land of the pine, the fig and the orange, started for California "across the plains," with ox-teams, in the spring of 1864. We joined a small party of friends from our immediate neighborhood, whose destination was Colorado. A short time previous to this the discovery of gold and silver mines at Pike's Peak had created a wild excitement, and as this was before the era of railroads in that region, the "Big Road" from the Missouri River was crowded with long trains of wagons, some bound for Denver, then a thriving town, and others for points still farther west. There was also a large emigration that year to the Pacific Coast. The war had caused an unsettled state of society, and many sought homes in those more quiet and peaceful countries. The emigrants of that time not only suffered the exposures, inconveniences and hardships incident to such a journey, but were momentarily in danger of being attacked by hordes of wild savages, through whose lands they passed.

We had not proceeded far on our journey before rumors of attacks from Indians in advance of us caused some anxiety. Our journey lay along the Platte River, and, as far as the eye could reach, it took in miles and miles of level land, green in the month of May, and skirted by hills and abrupt bluffs. These plains were the home of the wild cactus, and in many places their showy flowers beautified the lone, deserted landscape. At intervals of many miles, the dreariness of the long level road, the distant hills and capricious river, was broken by sight of a rude hut, inhabited by "a bold pioneer," one of those daring and adventurous spirits who recognize no such word as fear. The hut was usually built of sod, the sod of the plain cut in uniform shape and dried and put together after the manner of brick. It was the only available material for building purposes, and, built layer upon layer, offered a stout defense against the attacks of the wary and watchful foe. It was not infrequently the case that "the bold pioneer" made friends with the Indians by taking a wife from one of the most powerful tribes. Besides being a "stage station" for the regular overland stage, he carried on a brisk traffic with the Indians and white hunters and trappers in furs, hides and pelts, giving in exchange blankets, beads, etc., and *always whisky*, which latter found innumerable customers among the endless throng of thirsty emigrants.

We passed the pretty and picturesque Fort Cottonwood, the fortifications and buildings being built mostly of hewn cedar. The bluffs and cañons beyond the fort contained vast quantities of this beautiful timber. The fort was garrisoned by a small detachment of soldiers for the purpose of protecting travel and guarding the frontier. The overland stage at each station was provided with an escort of soldiers, who accompanied it from one station to another. It was not an uncommon occurrence for the soldiers in those journeys to be "picked off" or "taken in a surround" by the vigilant and ever wary foe; but it was a rare thing that an Indian was captured, dead or alive. A story was related of an Indian being captured the summer before, and, after being duly and very much scalped, was buried in a shallow grave. A squad of soldiers traveling that way were told of the achievement. Doubtful of its truth. they demanded to see the remains, and, on repairing to the spot, they unearthed the body and scalping it again, bore away the ghastly trophies in exultation.

On such a journey as that of crossing the plains, one grows weary of the unvarying monotony, the long days in the wagon, with its ceaseless creaking, and if with ox teams, the slow plodding of the oxen, the very voice of the driver, with his occasional, and scarcely necessary, "gee, gee, Brandy!" "haw, Buck, haw!" There is the long yellow road stretching for miles before us, the green sweep of plain, and the sombre hills flanking our left, while to the right runs (does it?) yes, sometimes, that questionable and doubtful river, the Platte. However, one of a sunny temperament, and fully determined, might contrive, on such a journey, to experience a degree of pleasantness, especially if in a large train, and with a jovial company. If a halt was ordered early, there was ample time for supper, the savory out-of-door odor of the cooking, gathering of the "buffalo chips,"—(does't it seem like an age since we crossed the plains?)—and after supper we restfully reclined on our blankets on the grass while the patriarchs, fearlessly and enjoyably smoked their pipes, and speculated on the new land to which we were journeying, the progress of the war, and its probable result; we, awed and made silent by the vastness of the untenanted dominions, looked around, saw the sunset fade away, the blue of the sky grow deeper, and the stars slowly shed their luster over the darkening earth. Among the fun-loving and less thoughtful at such times, the jest and song went round, and the sound of laughter and mirth penetrated the gloom and floated out and was lost in the grim darkness.

During the years of the civil war there was a heavy emigration across the plains from the south, and though many of them hated the "brave old flag," they were glad to seek peace and protection under its folds in the prosperous countries of the Pacific Coast. We chanced to camp one evening in close proximity to a large train of Southerners. It was near a station, and the stage having arrived there a short time before, brought the latest war news, which was in substance that a victory had been gained by some of the rebel forces. There was great rejoicing that night in the neighboring camp, and "Hurrah for *owa* side!" rang upon the air in lusty chorus.

Rumors of trains attacked by Indians reached us from time to time, and one day a band of painted warriors, hundreds in number, passed us. Two large powerfully built warriors, in all the glory of red paint, buckskin, beads, feathers, dignity and general magnificence, condescended to honor our humble camp with a call—a call long enough to eat up and devour everything we had cooked, that being an immense pot of beans and bacon, an astonishing amount of bread, a half bushel of cookies, about four pounds of crackers, cold potatoes, pickles, "and setery," too numerous to mention. We were glad when they left; we felt relieved, and we *were* relieved. Though they went away without paying their bill, we were glad when they departed and have scarcely ceased rejoicing yet. Had they continued to devour everything eatable an hour longer, with the same avidity as they did during those memorable fifteen minutes, not a soul in our camp would have been alive to-day to tell the tale. Though we suffered no personal attack, we afterwards learned that "the war had actually begun;" before us and behind us the murderous savages were committing their diabolical deeds.

I subsequently became acquainted with a lady who that same year crossed the plains, reaching Denver two weeks in advance of us. Their train was attacked by Indians, some of their number being killed; fortunately, she and her family escaped. Their party was a small one, consisting of their two wagons, in charge of her husband and brother, and two wagons loaded with merchandise, in charge of a man and his son. One day, while traveling along as usual without any thought of danger, her brother, whose wagon was just behind the one she occupied, stepped up to her wagon and got his rifle. She noticed the action and asked what was the matter? "Nothing, I hope," he replied, "only I don't like the looks of those dark objects just above the bluffs there." Looking in the direction he indicated she saw on the verge of the hills, some distance away, numerous dark objects, mere specks, outlined against the horizon. Scarcely had he ceased speaking, when up on the top of the hill there appeared in plain view a band of mounted warriors, and the next moment, swift as a shower of arrows, they swept down upon the little train. Her brother stood ready with his gun, but, circling past, they dashed on to the rear wagons, which contained merchandise. There they soon dispatched the drivers, killing both instantly; and unharnessing the mules, proceeded to load them with the contents of the wagons, which was flour, sugar, meat, etc. After plundering the wagons they mounted their ponies and, driving the mules before them, slowly trotted off over the bluffs.

When within about one hundred miles of Denver, we were witnesses of one of the most terrible rain and hail storms that ever visited the Platte region. It was a water spout or cloud burst. We afterwards ascertained that we were on the verge of the storm. As the rain and hail began to descend, we halted our wagons, and looking westward saw a black cloud resembling a horn of plenty emptying its contents in a fearful deluge. Hail stones of enormous size fell, striking with great force our dumb, unsheltered animals, and the vivid sheet lightning played with continuous glare on the covers of our wagons as though the elements were ablaze. After the storm was over, and we resumed our journey, we found some immense hail stones, one by actual measurement, was nearly three inches in diameter. We were not aware of the extent of the damage done by the storm, until, on reaching Denver, nearly two weeks after. We then learned that the water spout had emptied its contents on a portion of the city and vicinity, that the loss of property, of houses, fences and stock was enormous, and the loss of life considerable. Such was the force of the rain, that stock herders in the hills had scarcely time to reach a shelter, and in some instances were drowned; houses were floated off and wrecked. Cherry Creek was full of the debris, dismantled and half-submerged buildings—drowned stock, fences, etc.

Before arriving in Denver, we found that our teams were in such a condition as to be unfit to travel much farther; add to this the fact that the whole Indian country was aroused and arming against the whites, induced us to stop in Colorado, intending to stay during the winter and resume our journey to the Pacific Coast the following spring. As we neared our journey's end, the snow-tipped summits of Pike's and Long's Peaks in the Rocky Mountain range, each day became more distinct. Hidden from view by a roll of hills, and lying at the base of the mountains, was the active and growing town of Denver. We had decided, however, to proceed to the mines, and chose the vicinity of Black Hawk, Central City and Nevada as our place of destination. These three mining towns were forty miles from Denver, and located consecutively in a gulch. Camping for a short time in the verge of the city, it was pleasant to look once more upon the bright, attractive homes of civilization—hear the busy hum and stir of modern improvement, and feel the security and friendship that a settlement of our countrymen and kindred afforded.

Our rest was brief, and once more on the march, we soon enter the hill country. Our road lies through the pretty town of Golden City, an infant village merely. The country around it is broken—the miniature valleys abounding in grain ranches, stock ranches, etc. Ere long we penetrate the fastnesses of the "Rockies." I had been familiar with the kindly grandeur and sublime beauty of the Sierras, but what a contrast was here presented! For miles and miles our road led through deep, dark cañons walled on either side by solid rock, steep and perpendicular. Stunted pines and scant vegetation at times varied the barren scenery, and a clear stream flowed through the length of the cañon, along the banks of which many varieties of beautiful flowers hitherto unknown to me, bloomed in great profusion.

We soon found that Colorado differed from California in many respects. The mines, which were gold and silver quartz mostly, were owned generally by Eastern capitalists. The climate was severe and rigorous—subject to violent wind and snow storms, and intense cold. In certain seasons the wind howled and shrieked up and down the gulches and across the barren rocky ridges in furious blasts, often filling the air with the fine "tailings" or dust from the mines, and chips, bits of wood and pebbles would come clattering against the windows and sides of the houses, creating a perfect pandemonium. All articles of consumption—all supplies were transported across the plains, a distance of 600 miles, in wagons. During the winter, with every slight fall of snow, all articles of food advanced in price, especially such heavy articles as flour, meat, potatoes, etc. Flour at one time was $16 per sack; beef, 50 cents per pound; potatoes, 25 cents per pound, and all heavy articles in proportion. Vegetables of all kinds were very scarce and commanded a high price. Canned goods were the principal dependence. Colorado at that time was badly "grasshoppered," and for years and years was a sufferer from this merciless marauder. This was the prime cause of the high price of vegetables and home produce. The years of the civil war were perhaps the darkest in the history of Colorado since its settlement by the whites. Her means for conveying supplies were meagre and limited, and through a country that was swarming with hostile foes. Her forts were poorly garrisoned and the Indians roving on her vast plains committed unchecked depredations and outrages on the defenseless inhabitants.

At last the long and severe winter drew to a close, and with the advent of spring, balmy winds and soft sunshine, and beautiful flowers, the glad beams of peace illuminated the land. News of the fall of Richmond was telegraphed through the rocky wilds of this struggling, new country. Even in the heart of this wilderness the fires of patriotism burned fervently in the bosom of every loyal citizen, and great was the rejoicing when the news was received. Business of all kinds was suspended; miners came from the underground works and exchanged their mud begrimed suits for holiday attire. Quartz-mills were "shut down" and mining camps deserted, while towns and hamlets were decorated with banners and flags and every symbol of universal rejoicing.

At night the mountains were ablaze with illuminations, torchlight processions, bonfires, etc., and the steady booming of anvil and cannon reverberating through the fastnesses of the mountains proclaimed the dawn of peace.

Alas! how sudden is often the transition from joy to sorrow. Scarcely had the echoes of the cannon died away among the resounding peaks and rocky cañons, when closely following in the path of these great victories there came the mournful tidings of the assassination of President Lincoln—he who was alike the friend of the South as of the North. It seemed as though the pulse of the nation had ceased to beat. "The thunderbolt had fallen to the hearth," and the whole country put on the badge of mourning.

> "He was our standard bearer—he
> Caught up the thread of destiny
> And round the breaking Union bound
> And wove it firmly.
> * * * * * * * *
> The hand that signed the act of grace
> Which freed a wronged and tortured race."

Again was business suspended, but from a far different cause, and instead of the loud booming of cannon there was an ominous silence—a silence fraught with dark forebodings. Each one felt he had lost a personal friend.

CHAPTER XIV.

STILL ON THE WING—THE SUNSET LAND—A RAILROAD ACROSS THE CONTINENT.

In June, 1865, my husband joined a party which was formed for the purpose of prospecting for mines in the interior. He therefore determined to send his family "back East," and I once more found myself in company with a small party of returning emigrants, with our faces turned toward the land of the rising sun. Indian hostilities continued, and the Governor of the Territory had shortly before issued orders that all trains should travel twenty-five or more in a company. As soon as possible we joined with another train, and each night on going into camp formed the wagons into a corral and a guard was kept during the night; each man and woman carried weapons ready for defense. About sunset one day, we passed the ruins of the old American Ranch where a few months before a provision train of 80 wagons had been captured by the Indians, their drivers who did not escape by flight, were either killed or taken prisoners. After pillaging the wagons and taking what they desired, they burned the remainder; the ground was strewn with wagon tires, hubs and odd bits of iron.

It was said that during the attack two Indians had been killed, and their bodies left in the ruins of the old sod hut. We camped about two miles below the ruins, and two women belonging to the train, accompanied by several men, walked back that evening in order to see the carcasses of the dried up and "very dead braves." In describing them, they said that instead of decomposing, they merely dried up, their skin adhering to the bone and their hands and feet resembling claws. What horrible fascination induced them to walk those four long miles in order to feast their gaze on this revolting spectacle, I was unable to understand; as for myself, thoroughly wearied with life in the wilderness, I would gladly have traveled as far again to avoid their vicinity.

Being near the scene of recent murder and outrage, our little camp redoubled its watchfulness. Four men stood guard that night, and long after the hour of retiring, I laid awake thinking and looking at the stars through the window in my wagon—I could not sleep. The night was chilly, and a fire smoked and blazed near my wagon, around which the watchful and alert guard at times sat and talked. The conversation naturally, under the circumstances, centred on Indian stories, Indian attacks, crossing the plains, etc., and as the night wore on they grew more and more eloquent—it seemed to me they were gifted with an *awful* eloquence on that particular subject. Now and then one of the guards stole from the little group and patroled the camp. About midnight one of them came in and remarked: "I'm blest boys if I ain't afraid there's suthin skulkin' among the horses." A hasty look at their trusty rifles, and the four men started away to reconnoitre. I arose and looked out, wondered what I should do in case of an attack. Examined my pistol and saw it was loaded, looked at the form of a lady who occupied the wagon with me, and at the peaceful faces of my little children all quiet and undisturbed in slumber—sat and listened, and after what seemed to be an interminable length of time, the four men came back and quietly resumed their places by the fire. "Well," remarked a tall, saffron-colored, sandy whiskered fellow, "danged ef I didn't think I seed a hoss agoin acrost to the bluffs jest after we got out thar." "O dry up," came in reply; "we've got nervous tellin' our Injun yarns—but I say, Bill, sposin' we wus attacked, what *would* you do?" Bill, thus appealed to, straightened himself up and replied: "*Do?* By jingo I'd fight if I got cornered and had to, but I'd run if I could." Though the time, place and circumstances were little calculated to inspire mirth, I could not repress a smile at the simple frankness of Bill's reply, and though one might not give him credit for remarkable daring, we were prone to trust his veracity;—however, such frequently display most courage when it is most needed. One of the world's greatest generals once remarked when he saw an ashen-faced man marching up to a battery, "There goes a good soldier; give me a man who knows his danger and faces it without flinching." Bill certainly possessed one of these requisites—he seemed to comprehend thoroughly his danger. Needless to say there was little sleep for me that night, and it was with a feeling of relief and gratitude that I watched the slow approach of day, the indistinct streaks of the gray dawn, heard the first noisy stir of camp life, and saw the sun rise large and yellow, flooding the long stretches of tawny plains—and our hasty breakfasts being soon dispatched, our wagons slowly moved into line and stretched out on the long, dusty road.

We met one day a long train of Mormon proselytes bound for the kingdom of the "Latter Day Saints." Poor, ignorant and dirty—they seemed to be the dregs of some foreign country. As wagon after wagon rolled past us, and groups of men, women and children, barefooted, toiled on in the sand, numbers of our train saluted them with "I say, you're going the wrong way!" "Hallo there! better turn back old man!" and the like; but with their faces turned

Zionward, and the toes of their feet pointing toward the City of the Saints, they heeded not the scoffs and sneers of the unbelievers, and turning neither to the right nor to the left, kept stolidly on their way In direct contrast was a train of returning Mormons with whom we camped occasionally. They had escaped the terrors of the law and the "Avenging Angels," and after a residence of years in Zion, at last were *going home*. They conversed but little on the subject of Mormonism, but if one might judge from a casual observation, their souls seemed to have been steeped in the waters of Marah; the slightest reference made to the subject from time to time, convinced us that it stirred up a flood of painful and unpleasant recollections. There was one woman particularly whom I shall never forget—she had resided there fifteen years, and without doubt had had her share of bitter experience. Her face, her speech and very manner impressed us as one who had drank deeply of bitter waters.

With feelings of heartfelt gratitude for our safe journey, we entered the confines of civilization. A few months later my husband joined us, and locating in the town of B., on the Missouri River, we engaged in the photographing business. This section of the country is one of the most fertile and attractive portions of the State. The soil is rich and capable of producing all kinds of fruits, vegetables, cereals, etc., peculiar to this latitude. The country is beautiful, abounding in rolling hills, bluffs and prairies. The hills are covered with a dense growth of timber, and the rich dark woods abound in nuts of various kinds—hickory nuts, walnuts and hazel nuts; and along the streams are found wild plums in great profusion, and equaling the finest cultivated plum in delicacy of flavor—wild strawberries are also abundant, and gooseberries, etc. Notwithstanding the many attractions that surrounded us in this new home, our faithful hearts, which *could not forget*, were prone to turn in restless yearning to the land of the setting sun. Agreeable to the impulse, in November, 1869, we found ourselves once more westward bound, this time on the Transcontinental Railway.

THE SUNSET LAND.

Ah! many a morn when the earth is fair
 And the lark's wild song rings clear—
Sweet visions steal through the empty air,
 Away from the finished years—
  O, had I the wings
  Of the bird that sings—
I would speed o'er the trackless main,
  Where lingeringly
  By the sunset sea,
Those years I'd woo again.

And many an eve when the sky is bright,
 And the heavens are deeply blue,

And the wind swims up with a winsome light,
  And the stars shine brightly through—
    I dreamily
    Call back to me
A land on the sunset shore,
    Where wave dark pines
    Over hidden mines,
My feet hath pressed of yore.

Where the golden oriole plumed his wing,
  And the huntsman's horn was heard,
And the streamlet's voice in its wandering
  Was free as the proud, bright bird—
    On the mountain's crest
    In the far-off West
Was my home of the cherished past,
    Where swift and sweet
    Beneath my feet,
Life's flowers were thickly cast.

The flowers have dropped from youth's fair shrine,
  And the years will return no more,
But the fragrant breath of the murmuring wind
  Blows soft from that sunlit shore—
    And phantoms fair
    Through the viewless air,
Oppress me with regret,
    Sweet pictures come
    From lips now dumb,
Whose words I never can forget.

O, linger, winds! of the far-off land,
  And voices of buried times,
And blow ye waves from the golden strand,
  With the murmuring song of the pine,
    For unto me,
    Thy song shall be
A rhythm with memories rife—
    Whose melody
    Shall cling to me
To the sunset shores of life.

A railroad across the continent, which has been a reality over sixteen years, is now scarcely considered an achievement of more than ordinary interest, and like the transatlantic submarine cable, hardly awakens at this time more than a passing thought. But a quarter of a century ago those who entertained the theory as at all practicable were looked upon as mere enthusiastic visionaries. I remember when, at one time, I ventured to timidly predict that I should see the day—nay, *fervently hoped to cross the continent by railway*, my earnest remark was laughed to scorn, and I was doubtless considered an unreasoning visionary. There was at that time such a theory—but a theory which then seemed as impalpable and improbable as does, at the present, "Symmes' theory of the North Pole," and though it had its earnest supporters, the undertaking, so gigantic and full of peril, so difficult, and requiring such an enormous outlay of capital, was looked upon as an event which, if ever accomplished, would belong to the dim and remote future; one, perhaps, that our great-grand-children might possibly live to see, but which was beyond the pale of *our* destiny. But since that time what grand and glorious achievements have the fruitful years unfolded. From a prominent journal we quote: "At present there are seven overland railroads, either completed or in progress, to reach the Pacific Ocean; embracing four systems—the Central and Union Pacific, the new Atlantic and Pacific route, the Texas Pacific and Southern Pacific. The Denver and Rio Grande is pushing for this Coast, and the Chicago, Milwaukee and St. Paul railroad, which proposes to extend its line from Dacota to Pacific Ocean. The last spike was but a few weeks ago driven in the Northern Pacific and Canadian Pacific. Then there are two Mexican roads, which will soon span the Mexican portion of the continent, besides two ship canals projected."

CHAPTER XV.

ECHO CANYON, THE BEAUTIFUL—DEVIL'S GATE—THE HUMBOLDT
DESERT—THE MAIDEN'S GRAVE.

November 15*th*—A drizzling rain and lowering sky hovered above our departure. The ride to the station, distant some four miles, was uncomfortable in the extreme, but once on the train, we are fairly started. By six o'clock the same day we took the 'bus for the Council Bluffs depot for Omaha—just one hour too late for the westward bound train, and perforce must wait another day.

November 16*th*—At four o'clock we take a 'bus for the depot, and through mud and mire unlimited go slashing and splashing till at last we are set down at the depot, where, with many other impatient emigrants, we wait two mortal hours, then we hear a shriek, a puff, and the monster is gliding abreast the platform. Then "there is hurrying to and fro"—O, what a gathering of bundles and baskets, overcoats, lap-dogs, babies, guns!—everything portable—and what a rush, lest you may be left or be without a seat! As those things are items worthy of consideration, we join the general melee, and start for the cars. My husband takes the lead, bearing the provision trunk and shrub-box, while Ernest follows with a huge roll of blankets and a gun. Walter supports his gun and carpet sack triumphantly, and May and I are left to bring up the rear with the two little children and the two baskets, which we do right nobly. Some little distance has to be traversed, over railroad tracks and around freighted cars—and of all the funny sights! I haven't seen anything to equal it since I "crossed the Isthmus" in '54. Each man, woman and child loaded with their respective bundles, and all in a hurry! I got to laughing so that I was unable to get into the car; but, thanks to a gentleman, was assisted in. These are the second-class cars—$60 per ticket—and we carry our own provisions, which is no small item, as we are told that this will be our home for eight or ten days. So we smooth down our feathers and settle down quite comfortably, occupying as many seats as "the law allows us," for we are thinking of eight or ten nights when we shall have to improvise beds of the seats and our blankets. We throw aside all reserve and conventionalism, and are soon in friendly converse with several of our fellow-passengers. Some five or six ladies are in "our car"—intelligent, lively and sensible; while the gentlemen are agreeable and polite—sho! says conscience, as though the gentlemen were not everywhere agreeable and polite.

Soon the engine shrieks a final farewell through the gloom, and we realize that we are indeed on the grand continental railway, bound for the Pacific Coast (the third time)—that we have left friends and old associations—and, heedless of the din and clatter, the merry talk, the jokes and confusion, we find ourselves prone to indulge in tender recollections, but this must be put aside, for we have not yet had time for supper. So now, that we are fairly under way, the dinner baskets must be discussed. When bed time arrives, the car is crowded. Each person seeks to get himself into such a position as will be most likely to woo the drowsy god. Looking down the car, I notice that hats, boots and waterfalls occupy the most conspicuous positions, though many from choice—"Hobson's choice"—have taken a sitting position to secure a nap. Not much sleep visits our eyelids the first night, having occasionally been awakened by the jokes of the "boys" who were so unfortunate as to have given up their seats to the ladies. I feel a profound solicitude for those poor fellows, who to all appearances are doomed for eight or ten consecutive nights to vary the monotony of restless wanderings through the aisle with "roosting" on the backs of seats; but the way of the emigrant is hard, and the "wee sma' hours" of night are kept noisy by sleepy jokes.

November 17*th*—We look out and see the long level stretch of Platte bottom. Certainly so far this is one of the most favorable railway routes in the world—almost a dead level, from the Missouri to the mountains. We are getting on finely—a nice, warm car, soft cushioned seats, good lights, good fires and plenty of water, though not very good. Conductor keeps clear and we're "masters of the situation."

November 18*th* — CHEYENNE — A pretty little town, 516 miles from Omaha. No end to hotels, eating saloons, drinking saloons, etc., while in the distance I saw some two or three neat and beautiful churches. It is a town of two or three years' growth, containing several thousand inhabitants. It is perfectly surprising! Situated in the heart of the wilderness— hundreds of miles from civilization—a young city blessed with neat churches, schools, business houses and pretty residences, etc. Verily to hear is to doubt, but to see is to believe.

> "I hear the tramp, the mighty tread
>   Of nations yet to be—
> The first low wash of waves where soon
>   Shall roll a human sea."

And seeing the march of civilization in this young city of the wilderness, we hear the voice of the mighty waves of emigration beating and surging against its rocky strongholds.

At Antelope a second storm overtook us. It blew in wild gusts and eventuated in a snow storm. The snow is now three or four inches deep but the afternoon sun is shining warm and radiantly. We are now on the eighteen-mile grade, said to be the most dangerous grade on the whole route. Every ten miles, "more or less," as the lawyers say, we pass a station house where a man is constantly employed to inspect ten miles of the road and keep it in order. They are scattering human habitations—the distant outposts of civilization.

November 19*th*.—Carefully and slowly last night we came up the long grade which terminated at Sherman—the summit—the highest point on the route, reaching an altitude of 8,000 feet above sea level. And now for the down-grade, steeper than the up-hill. I have never experienced a more exciting ride. It is fearfully sublime! We skim the ground—we fly! We fly through strips of seemingly level plain, through deep cuts whose frowning and overhanging rocks project directly above us. It is a lovely moonlight night, rendered still more beautiful by the ground being covered with snow. Through all this long, swift ride I held my baby fast gathered in my arms. What if some overhanging, treacherous rock had slipped its fastening and rolled upon the track? What if—a thousand things. Away! I will not dream of these. God's hand that stilled the tempest is with us as the iron horse with its precious freight thunders across the Rocky Mountains. What a sense of relief I experience when the long twenty-mile grade is past; a grade of eighty feet to the mile. We draw a long breath, for we have passed some frightful places during the fearful ride. At one time the train stopped in the middle of a rocky ridge, on either side of which was a deep, yawning chasm. Now and then the engine started with a jerk, then backed again, still keeping us in this uncomfortable position, while the storm without howling and surging and thundering against the cars, rocked us as in a cradle, suggesting terrible thoughts. But at last we passed safely over the frightful causeway. We have passed Laramie, a very nice little town, besides many other little stations of lesser importance.

We can scarcely believe that we are in the Mountains, for around us on either side are smooth, unbroken plains as if designed by nature for the path of the iron horse. Afar, on the left, the deep blue swell of the Wind River mountains is plainly visible. It is clear and beautiful, though rather cold weather to-day, and the clouds are hurled back against the horizon. We go on at a good swinging pace; expect soon to be in Promontory. Our journey has been enlivened by herds of deer, antelope, and elk, also badgers and wolves—no buffaloes. The song of bird is seldom heard along the tarack.

November 20—A most lovely day. The pet canaries in my neighbor's cage are reveling in the warm sushine. We are at Wahsatch, 116 miles from Promontory. I hear the men sounding the car wheels, which is done every fifty miles, the engine is also changed every fifty miles. A number of boys have boarded the train, selling bread, cakes, coffee, etc.; bread twenty-five cents per loaf, coffee ten cents per cup. We are going through romantic and picturesque scenery. Bear River, clear and murmuring, over a pebbly bed is a lovely little stream. At noon we enter Echo Cañon, the beautiful. A romantic natural defile, some 100 feet wide by 17 miles long, the mountains on either side, tall and majestic, are of red sandstone abounding in rocky ridges and covered with tamarac and sage brush, and bearing unmistakable evidence of having been worn by the action of waters, years, perhaps centuries ago. It is picturesque beyond description—the long, level dell through which a clear stream ripples and wanders, and the frequent occurrence of warm springs, around and near which the green grass grows in all the luxuriance of early June. Here on the very summits of these loftiest peaks we see the remains of ancient breastworks built years ago by the Mormons under Brigham Young, in order to shoot down on the Government troops which were sent out by Uncle Sam in 1857 to suppress Mormonism.

These enduring breastworks, situated as they are on the tops of these loftiest peaks, recall to the peaceful traveler a scrap of frontier history which is interesting in the extreme. For many a long year they will remain a monument to the failure of an attempt to crush out a "peculiar society," which for its abominable practices and outrageous creeds and its ignorant and fanatical followers, has no similarity in the world's history. They seem to recall to mind the millions of wasted army munitions and treasury funds, and the utter failure of that memorable attempt.

Weber River, running through the cañon is clear and full of mountain trout. We have stopped at Echo City, a small hamlet. Here we bought some Utah apples—fruit of a superior quality. This is a lovely spot. We have passed several Mormon villages, and I notice two features which seem to be characteristic of this "peculiar" society, to-wit: the utter and hopeless poverty of the people, and the number of children. Judging from the number of little, tow-headed saints that swarm about the low log huts, we come to the conclusion that this must be a "manufacturing" village. At sunset we near the renowned natural wonder, called Devil's Gate.

History and tradition have made us familiar with this remarkable and awe-inspiring place. Huge mountains frown narrowingly on either side, at the base of which a deep and rugged hole seems to have been scraped by demon claws. The mountains of solid rock descend almost perpendicularly, and at the very bottom of the gorge the Weber River, deep and dark tumbles among the rugged rocks. The railroad track spans the wide and gloomy gorge.

Slowly we pass above and look from the dizzy height—only a narrow railroad bridge on which to cross this "Witch's Cauldron."

Not the least interesting feature of this awe-inspiring and wonderful place is the old emigrant road. Far below it winds its course around the margin of the river, a worn and yellow track. At one point, where the mountains descend abruptly nearly to the river brink, the solid rock has been picked and hewn away as if by painful labor, until there is, by careful driving, just room for a wagon to pass; above hang the jutting frowning rocks, and below rolls the deep dark river. How many wearied teams have passed under that shelving cliff! How many toil-worn travelers have shuddered in fear and terror as they passed beneath the shadow of this threatening mass of rock! How many human skeletons lie whitening in the deeps of this dark river! The river tells us not in its unconscious murmurings, the wind brings no wispers in its wild ravings, and the stony mountains bear no record on their frowning fronts; but we recall to memory stray stories of the sufferings of the early emigrants—of lost stock, wrecked wagons, and dead men's bones—that haunt this awful "Devil's Gap." We pass on, and a sigh of relief escapes us as the last car rolls past the gorge, and we emerge from Echo Cañon into an open plain, bounded by stupendous mountains, whose view is shortly cut off by the gloom of gathering night. But I cannot leave the cañon without allowing my pen to linger over the record of a most rare and beautiful sight. It was about three o'clock, the day fair and sunny, at a point where the mountains reared their stupendous heights on either side, and covered the cañon with shadow. In the deep shadow I saw above me glimmering in the clear transparent air a single large and lovely star! Star of the daylight in the Rocky Mountains! Was there another one that saw it? I shall accept it as a harbinger of future good.

Since leaving the Black Hills the weather has been warm and pleasant. During the night we pass a very interesting portion of our journey—Ogden, quite a nice city bordering on Salt Lake, also Corinne and Promontory. At the last named place we change cars and speed on. The shadows of night are around us, and on we go; while close upon our left the dim far stretching water of the Great Salt Lake repose and glimmer in the starlight. Many regrets are expressed that we could not have viewed the great interior basin by day.

November 21*st*.—Daylight finds us speeding over the Desert. The country presents a level tract of land, bounded on either side by grand majestic mountains. The soil is strongly impregnated with alkali. Sage brush and greasewood with occasional patches of wild rye, are the only vegetation. The weather during the day is warm and pleasant, at night it is freezing cold. We pass "section houses," Chinese camps, and eating saloons, all board shanties. We see a few Indians, the only ones we have seen on the journey, begging at the camps.

Passed Elko last night; a pretty little town; regretted it was at night. Here runners came into the cars, bringing apples, pears and grapes; the finest fruit I ever saw. We have had a perfect feast, and all the small emigrants are perfectly delighted. We go on safely and easily making our eight or ten miles an hour. Halted at ten o'clock long enough to allow the gentlemen to take a bath in a warm spring, the steam of which was plainly visible a few hundred yards off in Humboldt Valley. A fellow passenger, an old gentleman seventy years of age, remarked when he saw the passengers running to the spring through the thick sage brush, "I don't see what they want to run away out there for, a scuffin out their boots."

Heigho, what fun the conductor made last evening. He is a jovial, hearty soul, and kept us awake with his jokes. He is an exception to the generally recognized assertion that "Conductors are the meanest men in the world."

November 22d—Had a nice time this morning, got out with a small party and took breakfast at Winnemucca; fresh biscuits, buckwheat cakes, ham and eggs, tea and coffee, sweet potatoes, Irish ditto, butter, pies, fruit, etc., meals 50cts; "meals at all hours and accommodations for one," besides the landlord gave us a *new Frank Leslie's Illustrated*. Nice landlord! good breakfast! will patronize him every time we come this way. We are soon under way again, while the same seemingly endless monotony of sage brush and greasewood covers the broad valley, and the mountains repose silently in the distance. Along the track where the ground has been thrown up, the soil has an ashen-gray appearance, as though the country had at some day in the far past been deluged in burning lava, and is at present the silent witness of a volcanic eruption. Strange country, desolate and uninviting! I am anxious to see what will come after this long, monotonous valley of the Humboldt.

How many fine views we pass in the night. Last night we passed that romantic spot, The Maiden's Grave. An emigrant girl was buried there long years ago, her grave left with only a rough board to mark the spot, but when the hardy men of California came to lay "the shining track of steely rails," they enclosed the sacred spot with a neat stone fence and placed a stone cross at the head, the symbol of Christianity—the act was touching and praiseworthy. The spot is pointed out and the history recited, but how many, alas! how many, sleep that dreamless sleep, their graves unknown and their very names almost forgotten? How many similar histories of broken hearts and desolate, sorrowing homes and wrecked hopes are brought forcibly to our faithful memories by the touching sight of the maiden's grave?

We are now within one day's travel of Sacramento. How near it seems, and yet how far! It is a most lovely day, the sun shines with dazzling lustre, the heavens are a dreamy blue, the brown valley stretches far and level, with near pictures of brown mountains and distant views of tall, blue peaks that lift their brows far up in the clear air and seem to kiss the skies.

Afternoon—We are at Humboldt City, and behind in the mountains we can see the mines —faint indications of the feeble powers of man in striving to wrench from the bowels of the adamantine rocks, earth's precious gems. We now pass a spot where some Chinamen are delving in the ground and bringing out sulphur. It looks like the pure article. We wonder if his Satanic Majesty wears a pigtail, and we feel easier when we glide past the spot, prolific with brimstone and imps with pigtails and almond eyes.

November 23d—When we awoke this morning the grand, beautiful scenery of California greeted our vision. Breakfast at Truckee, a pleasant looking town of 2,000 inhabitants. The view is essentially Californian. It looks like home and smells like home. Hail Oro! How familiar look the tall sloping mountains, covered with beautiful evergreens, and valleys through which murmur sparkling streams. We realize we are nearing home, that our journey is nearly at an end, and with what happy hearts we look out as the train speeds onward. We are now nearing the summit of the track reaching an altitude of 7,042 feet, descending at the rate of 90 feet to the mile; we go down 500 feet in six miles. The scenery is grand beyond description; we feel like we are on the "great backbone of earth." Here on the lofty summits of the Sierra Nevada, men were tied—it was necessary to secure them by tying them with ropes until they could pick a foothold in the solid, sloping rocks—and inch by inch the granite was picked away till a roadway was made, and after an enormous outlay of money and toil and engineering and brain work, the grand Continental Railroad was a success! I look down from this awful height and see the tops of tall pine trees, which appear dwarfed and insignificant, and a stream goes on its winding way, which looks like a silver thread. It is by far the grandest, most fearfully sublime portion of the road, but much of the view is shut off by snow sheds which are very substantially built to ward off the avalanche from the overhanging mountain. We pass through numerous tunnels. Snow sheds and tunnels are so closely connected, that we scarcely realize when we emerge from a tunnel into a snow shed. A momentary glimpse of green mountain peaks, frowning rocks and dark cañons, and we glide into darkness and gloom. Around rocky points thousands of feet above green valleys and murmuring rivers the train speeds on, and now the summit is reached and passed, and we are on the down' grade, another wild and fearful ride. Words fail to express our sensations. It is the sublimity of grandeur, wild and grand beyond description, far as the eye can see, the dark blue mountains are rolled range upon range, and crest upon crest.

We arrived at Colfax about five o'clock, 50 miles from Sacramento; we will be at our journey's end to-night. The mountains begin to present a spring-like appearance. The tender grass reminds us of May showers and sunshine. Cottages are scattered about, and hamlets reposing in dreamy green valleys; we see green peas and cabbage plants in the gardens. We are now in Placer County—the scenery is lovely. What a transition from that of two days ago. The monotonous wastes of the Humboldt have given place to spring-time verdure, rippling streams, gardens, vineyards, etc. On speeds the train to Sacramento, where we arrived safely last night at 12 o'clock, November 24th, 1869. We were eight days and six hours on the journey, and with heartfelt thanks for our safety, we rest after our long and fatiguing trip.

We look around us and feel the soft, balmy atmosphere, the warm rays of the genial sunshine, and though it is rainy winter, flowers are still growing and blooming in the garden-beds, the verandahs of residences are yet green and lovely with vine and bloom—in striking contrast is the severe, cold, drizzling November weather we left just eight days ago.

CHAPTER XVI.

BERRYESSA VALLEY—THE DEVIL'S GATE—PLEASANT VALLEY—A NIGHT UNDER THE SKY—GRAND ISLAND—A PICTURESQUE VALLEY—THE HAUNTED DELL.

A few weeks spent in patient search for a location for a home, and at last Berryessa Valley, in Napa County, was selected. Here we arrived on the 2d of January, 1870, glad to rest from wearisome journeyings, and happy to feel that we were once more settled, *and at home.*

Napa County has been appropriately and justly called one of the garden spots of California. It is rich and fertile, abounding in beautiful valleys divided by mountain ridges, which afford excellent pasture for stock. It has long been noted for its equable and pleasant climate. The soil is well adapted to all agricultural purposes. In many favored localities tropical fruits flourish. Napa Valley—the largest and oldest settled valley in the county, is in itself a gem of loveliness. What nature may have failed to do for this romantic and lovely vale, has been more than atoned for by the wealth, industry and enterprise of man.

Berryessa Valley, distant from Napa City some 26 miles, was until within the last fifteen years, the home of native Californians—the

Berryessa Bros., from whom it takes its name. Previous to its settlement and purchase by Americans, it was the "Rancho De Las Putas," the property of the wealthy and luxurious Spaniard. The lingering remnants of its once wealthy and powerful owners still reside, broken in fortune and thinned in numbers, on a small portion of their once vast possessions. At sight of them, handsome and commanding, and still gifted with the dark beauty of their race, one is led back in imagination to those primeval days. The valley was then little else but a wilderness of verdure—over whose vast pasture land roamed herds of horses and cattle, where the native grasses waved so high as to hide in their waving verdure the bands of cattle that fed thereon. A few adobe dwellings, staunch built and comfortable, were the only marked evidences of a semi-civilization. Numerous Indian villages along the banks of streams enlivened the solitude; deer, bear and other animals abounded in the surrounding mountains. Here, dreamed away in listless and luxuriant ease, the lordly Don, and his numberless retainers, the dusky Diggers. The sun rose and set, year after year, on the same scene—the same verdure of spring and tawny glint of autumn. Troops of dusky Indians lounged on their rancherias, mashed their acorns in rude stone bowls, and broiled their steaming venison or bear meat by the smoking fires near their wigwams, and with no thought of the future, and no warning dream of the encroaching footsteps of the pale faces, cared for no improvement and desired no change. But a land so gifted and so glorious, could not slumber long, unawakened by the "march of empire." The echo of its footsteps resounded on her border, and every leaf and blade of grass, and breath of wind, stirred to the sound. Before its resistless strides the native Californian and his belongings vanished like the dew of yestermorn. And lo! we see before us what a change the fruitful years have wrought! There are long lines of fences—vast fields of grain and corn—homes of wealth, beauty and refinement—and herds of cattle and horses and flocks of sheep feed on the green hill pasture. For miles the valley is level as a floor, without hill or hollow, and save the numerous "weeping oaks," presents an open scene of beauty and prosperity. Through its entire length flows a crystal stream, and in its centre is the quaint and pretty village of Monticello. For a period of ten years this beautiful valley was our home.

It was midsummer—the early morning cool and balmy—and in company with a small party of friends with capacious vehicle and camping outfit, we were intent on a protracted journey for the purpose of visiting friends in the neighboring county. Down the cañon, which is the natural outlet of Berryessa Valley, we made good time. The morning air was laden with the delicious perfume of wild grape blooms, wild roses, and the flashing waters of the crystal stream of Putah. On either side, the mountains, grand and imposing, reared their peak-like battlements. A ride of a few miles brought us to the Devil's Gate, a ponderous mass of boulders, between which the old road of Putah Cañon formerly ran. A sulphur spring in the vicinity, from which we drank, and which, when coupled with the Satanic title of the gate, was strongly suggestive of a very hot climate and things not pleasant to contemplate. Here is the dividing line of Napa and Yolo counties. It is written in large, white letters on the black face of the rock, and at the right, a corner of Solano county juts out in a huge mass of mountainous rock.

A few miles further on, we pass the vegetable farms in the vicinity of Pleasant Valley. Here grow the earliest vegetables that are taken to the San Francisco markets. Acres and acres of tomatoes, beans, squashes, etc., are to be seen, with bands of Chinese gathering them.

Turning a point, we sweep over undulating hills, and are in full view of a young city of the plain—Winters, a town of some two or three years' growth, but for two seasons the terminus of the Vaca Valley Railroad. Passing. thence our course lies northward—on the broad plain of the Sacramento Valley, devoid of tree or shrub, but one vast, endless grainfield. The eye rests on many substantial farmhouses with groves of orchards and green vineyards—others are mere tenant houses, small, and dark and dreary looking, and all glinting and glowing in the hot rays of a July sun. But beyond and far, what do we behold?—a crystal lake of clear, transparent waters, in which the reflections of grain-stacks and houses were plainly visible. We urge our steeds onward. Let us bathe the hot eyes and cool the burning brow in the limpid waters of the beautiful lake! The vision fades, it is only the mirage of the plains. Years ago, tired and thirsty, how oft we saw the same thing on the Colorado deserts, where in the limitless expanse of land and sky it lured the thirsty traveler on—a very *ignis fatuus*. Ere long, a more cheering feature of country is seen—we enter a beautiful belt of forest land, and hail with pleasure the inviting shades and sweet winds that sweep through the woods. Such droves of rabbits and hare scampering and galloping in every direction, and the air is vocal with the songs of birds.

As night closed around us, we sought a farm house where we procured hay for our horses, and selecting a pleasant camping spot, ordered a halt. How grateful was the odor of the delicious coffee and broiling steak in the open air, but weary of the long day's ride, we soon sought slumber—our only canopy the blue, dark vault above. The line of light in the western horizon is fading—far off we hear the lonesome "too whit, too whoo" of an owl. The sound of the horses munching their hay, and the sleepy note of some drowsy bird borne on the invigorating night wind greet the ear. There is a short prayer breathed for the loved ones at home, a thought of the dear old friends at the end of our journey, a dim gleam of the wonders of God's creation, with the words "The heavens declare the glory of God and the firmament showeth his handiwork"—then sense and sound are lost, and we drop into forgetfulness. The clarion notes of the morning bird at the gray dawn, roused us from a long, restful sleep. How strangely, brightly beautiful the stars shone down over the dark bosom of the slumbering earth! How cool and sweet came the morning wind, bearing in its low whispers the variable noises of awakening nature! Breakfast soon over, and we resume our journey. The broad Sacramento valley was before and around us. In the distance a timbered line of dark, green trees showed where the noble river ran. Beyond were the "Buttes," bold, rocky and awe-inspiring, and in the background, dim and almost undefinable, we saw the faint outline of the beloved Sierras! my first view of them for many years. Entranced by the view, and lost in pleasant recollections of bygone times, we scarcely heeded the time, till the pretty little village of College City was in sight, with its handsome church spire and neat private residences. The land in the vicinity was formerly a large sheep pasture, and owned by a gentleman—Mr. Pierce. Dying, he left his property for the purpose of building a church and college—which is known as Pierce Christian College, and for its age and location is one of the finest institutions of learning in the country. We passed the handsome little church, in the grounds of which repose the remains of this friend of humanity. There is a modest marble monument over the grave, but the work planned by his brain, and dictated by his heart, will live long after the marble has perished—its influence for good will be felt for generations.

Northward and towards the bluffs we now direct our course—where we know warm hands and loving hearts are waiting to give us welcome.

Two days later, and with some friends we are journeying towards Grand Island, a grand sweep of open country, with the bold Buttes in front and the dark line of trees margining the river growing nearer.

> And through the soft sun-lighted air,
> We see the mists that hover where
> The river's margined bosom lies.

We go through grain fields, pass corn patches, and cosy little cottages nestled deep among gigantic sycamore and oak trees, ere we reach the slough on the other side of which dwell those old companions of our early years. The bridge is crossed—the gate is opened, and though nearly eighteen years have passed since we stood face to face, the cordial grasp of the hand and the hearty welcome, assure us that time has not so completely wrecked our once youthful looks, but that the resemblance can be traced. We find here Mr. and Mrs. Stephen Burtis, the brothers M. and G. Stinchfield and Wm. Wright—old Nevada miners twenty years ago, who were for many years our old-time friends and companions. Time has dealt kindly with them, and though there are a few gray hairs, and a few lines of care that were not there twenty years ago, the hearts are still young and true to old friendships. Truly, "there is naught on earth more beautiful, or excellent, or fair, than the face of a friend," and a friendship that survives the wrecks and misfortunes and disasters of two decades, is "better than diamonds." Here we spent a day under the generous shade of the sycamore, recounting old scenes and memories, rambling in the beautiful woods where we cut our names on the bark of a grand, old tree, unmindful meanwhile, that our ages were counting up among the 40's, the 50's, and even the 60's. But time sped away, and with many a kind good by and promise to meet again, the morning sun found us homeward bound.

THE MEETING.

A golden day, sunbright and fair—
  A broad expanse of land and sky—
And thro' the soft, sun-lighted air,
We saw the mists that hover where
  The river's margined bosom lies.

We drifted down through fields of light—
  Our gallant steeds still bore us on,
From the far bluffs, now dim and white,
Toward the river darkly bright—
  Toward the Island's belted zone.

I'd tarried long in distant lands,
  And years had swiftly come and gone,
Since last I clasped the friendly hand—
Since last I met the olden band,
  Where breathes the pine's low monotone.

But strong desire now nerved me on,
  To greet the dear old friends of yore—
While fainter grows the hills beyond,
And nearer the enchanting bound—
  The Island fringed with sycamore.

We reach the bridge—unbar the gate—
  We gaze into each other's eyes,
And hands that sundered long by Fate,
Now clasp, tho' life is growing late,
  And smiles come up in glad surprise.

A long, sweet day in summer's prime,
  We spent amid the grand, old trees,
And backward, to the olden time
We wandered—while the low, sweet chime
  Of long ago, came on the breeze.

Just as we did so long ago,
  We wandered through the deep, dark woods,
We watched the shadows come and go—
We heard the wind sing soft and low,
  The charms of Nature's solitudes.

But night threw her unwelcome spell,
  Along the Island's girdled shore
Something upon our spirits fell—
We knew that soon the word—*farewell*
  From heart to heart would echo o'er.

Crossing the western boundary of Berryessa Valley and traversing the graded road, a distance of ten or twelve miles, we enter another of Napa County's most beautiful valleys, Pope Valley, and for diversified and picturesque scenery it is perhaps the most interesting and romantic. Fields of level land and belts of rich woodlands are broken by hills and elevations crowned with verdure. Beautiful winding roads cross and intersect each other in bewildering mazes, and clear, sparkling streams from the cool depths of the mountain fastnesses wind through the vale. In riding through the valley, one is continually being surprised by the charming glimpses of home-life and fascinating rural pictures disclosed to view. Rural villas and residences of wealth and beauty nestle among the mountain and forest streams, and grain fields, and orchards, while the green hills covered with flocks and herds, contribute to make a scene most charming and perfect.

>
Fair vale of the mountain!
>With its streamlets and fountains,
>And fields that grow green 'neath the touch of the sun,
>Where the cool oaken shadows
>Fall aslant on the meadows,
>And the winds weave a rhythm with the bees' drowsy hum.

This quiet and lovely vale is surrounded by points of more than passing interest. In its immediate boundaries are located some of the most popular health retreats and summer resorts on the Coast. The quicksilver mines are also located near. But the most interesting, and certainly the most fascinating attraction in the vicinity, is the mountainous chain that separates the valleys of Pope and Napa.

It differs from the ordinary Coast Range hills in soil, climate, productions, water, etc., and is simply one of those wonders of a wonder-abounding State. Here tower the finest specimens of forest trees, the lofty redwood, the stately pine, the fir, the beautiful madroña, and numerous other species of forest growth. The soil is deep and fertile and adapted to the cultivation of vineyards and fruits of all kinds. The climate is unrivalled in uniformity and kindliness of temperature. Cold springs abound, and numerous mountain streams, clear and sparkling, flow through cañons and plateau, often forming picturesque and romantic waterfalls and cascades. One of the most beautiful is Æolian Falls, situated in the depths of a dark forest—and some 60 feet in height. In early spring when the stream is swollen, the large body of water taking a sheer leap over the perpendicular precipice, tumbles in foam and spray into the miniature lake, filling the chasm with a deafening roar, and speeding onward takes its noisy way down through the cañon. Around and above, the mountains tower their green, moss-covered sides and forest-crowned summits.

Down in the heart of an evergreen forest,
    Where the dark shadows hang heavy and deep,
And the winds in their wantonness sport thro' the treetops,
    While murmurs the streamlet in musical sweep—
There is the realm of the naiads and fairies,
    'Mid the tall grasses, the ferns and the blooms—
Their laughter and song float in mystical echoes,
    And mingle their music with rarest perfume.

Ah! sweet as the dream of a poet's delusion,
    And fair as the castles we build in the air,
Is this dell in the forest in lovely seclusion,
    The home of the naiads and the tryst of the fair;

Far up from my perch where the mountain pine quivers,
   I watch and I listen, entranced by the spell
Of the echoes that ring on the miniature river,
   That's lost in the shadows that droop o'er the dell.

I hear their sweet laughter with snatches of singing—
   Of "tra-la-la-la"—"Come Will" and "Come Sue,"
"Press forward" and "hasten!" their echoes are ringing,
   And fainter in answer "We're following you,"
"Ah, tarry awhile"—come the voices entreating,
   "We're lingering to rest in this beautiful dell—
Where the ferns and the mosses and wild rose in greeting
   Have flung 'round the spot their bewildering spell."

And mid the dense leaflets by winds tossed asunder,
   I catch a rare vision of maiden or—sprite?
They repose on soft mosses of velvety wonder,
   Or chase the swift humming bird brilliant with light;
Still upward, and clearly their voices are floating,
   As if heedless of aught save the 'wild'ring hours—
As happy and glad in their gay, careless sporting,
   As the elfins themselves that inhabit the flowers.

I know the sweet spot that Nature hath vested
   With the deepest of shadows and brightest of sheen,
For there has my sad heart and weary feet rested,
   As I listened, entranced by the charm of the scene—
For sweet as the dream of a poet's delusion,
   And fair as the castles we build in the air,
Is this dell in the forest in lovely seclusion,
   The haunt of the naiad, and the tryst of the fair.

Here on the northern slope of this evergreen mountain in the salubrious climate of the Thermal Belt, surrounded by charming and romantic scenery—and with little to disturb the tranquillity but the voices of nature, is the home of the writer, "Arcadian Heights." The air is freighted with the rich aroma of pine, fir, redwood and other species of resinous wood; and the water, clear and soft, is unsurpassed. Until within a few short years ago, the mountain was a dense forest, the home and the abode of deer, bear and other animals—but it is now rapidly being redeemed from its primeval state, and converted into pleasant and comfortable homes. We who now plant orchards, vineyards, olive groves, etc., are but the second wave that follows in the van of civilization — we toil and we delve, and unearth the hidden germs of the soil. But shall there not come after us — following in the road our toil has hewn, those who, wiser, shall hold in their possession the mystic key that will unlock hidden treasures and lay bare avenues of wealth of whose splendor and magnificence we, in our little day, have never dreamed? Who can tell?

> O, give me a home in the wildwood,
>   Where the free bird singeth ever,
> Where the moss-grown bank of the forest glade
>   Hangs over the rushing river,
> And the grand old trees of the western land
>   Shall stand by my cot forever.
>
> And there by the forest's darkling rim,
>   Lit up by the sun's soft splendor,
> I love to live—and I live to love,
>   With a heart as light and tender
> As the birds themselves, whose winsome songs
>   Sweet homage unto me render.

I dream where the wild flowers softly blow,
   And the tall pines darkly quiver—
And I rove where the rustling western wind,
   Thro' the redwood wildly shivers,
And I love the sound, for Nature's voice
   So singeth her songs forever.

And nearer upward my soul is drawn,
   To the home of the one Eternal,
Whose many mansions no eye hath seen
   In the land of the Supernal,
Over whose fair flowers no blight is cast,
   Whose fields are forever vernal.

Oh! what were the world's proud boast of wealth,
   Or its fever-dreams of glory—
To peace and rest in the wildwood's breast,
   With the dark trees bending o'er me,
While lips I love and hearts that are true,
   Breathe ever the old, sweet story.

CHAPTER XVII.

RETROSPECTION — CONCLUSION.

During the last thirty years, since 1854, the time at which our story opens, have occurred some of the most remarkable events in the world's history—scientific discoveries, wonderful inventions, and the rapid progress and development of civilization in its onward march. Scarcely sixteen years have passed since the completion of that stupendous work—the Central and Union Pacific Railroad across the continent. It was the initial step in opening up to civilization the immense West; but until its commencement and completion the success of the undertaking, by the mass of people was considered impracticable. The Atlantic Cable also takes a front rank among the remarkable achievements embraced in that period. It too had its hosts of doubters and scoffers, both in the old world and the new, and the full glory of its success was scarcely dreamed of, even by the gifted brain that conceived it. The idea appeared to the world unreasonable and impossible that a submarine cable could be made so strong as to reach from continent to continent, so durable and impervious as to resist the action of salt water and the natural enemies of the deep—and could for any considerable time be kept in working order. Previous to that time it had required weeks and even months for news to reach us from the old world. Had we been told then that the news from England, speeches delivered in Parliament, the state of Her Majesty's health, etc., could reach us in the short space of eight or ten hours, the statement would have seemed highly absurd.

The little instrument, the telephone, though of recent invention, and so universally used and well known, is deserving of mention as being one of the remarkable scientific inventions of the past few years. The theory appeared to many as that of a cracked-brained visionary. The idea of holding audible converse with persons hundreds of miles away by means of a simple instrument inserted in a hole in the wall of a building and connected with others by a simple wire. It was all too simple and absurd, and simple people could not understand, and the simple world looked on and smiled, until a plain unpretending man demonstrated it and made it a grand success. Now every city and town of any importance has its regular telephone companies.

The electric light, too, that beautiful, brilliant, clear illumination, is among the most recent discoveries.

We who live in the light and enjoy the advantages and conveniences of these and many other grand developments of the last three decades, little comprehend the state of things —the Egyptian darkness, so to speak, in which our grandfathers dumbly groped, and the dusk shadows of which we of middle age distinctly remember. One which we realize as one of the most important things that has had a bearing on the progress and enlightenment of the present time, is the steam printing press. Through its means general intelligence and knowledge have been widely and generously distributed. It does not require a remarkable memory nor a very old person, to look back to the time when books were rare and beyond the reach of the masses. Newspapers and periodicals were like angels' visits, "few and far between." Printing presses were only in large cities and towns, and only hand presses were in use. How is it now? The steam printing press has become a mighty power in the land, disseminating knowledge and intelligence from all parts of the world in countless books, periodicals, newspapers, etc. By the general and cheap distribution of intelligence, it has been the means of opening the door to thought, to invention, and to the giant strides which progress and improvement have made, not only in the western countries, but in the world.

The American people are known as a reading nation, and consequently a thinking nation. To them belong many of the scientific discoveries and inventions of note which have been opened to the world in the last fifty years. But rapid as has been the advance of progress and improvement in this direction, it has only been equalled by the development and civilization of the West.

THE GREAT WEST.

What was the great west, that immense country lying beyond and west of the Father-of-waters fifty—nay thirty years ago? An interminable and almost untrodden wilderness. Many of us remember, and smile as we recall the picture that in our earlier geographies, across a large portion of that interior country was written in bold capital letters— UNEXPLORED. Previous to the year 1849, only a few daring spirits, hunters, trappers and adventurers had possessed the hardihood to push through the almost insurmountable barriers, and reach the Pacific Coast. Before the dawn of the age of gold in California, what was known of the countries of Dakota, Montana, Idaho and Oregon? They were with little exception an unknown wilderness, uncivilized and from their very nature uninhabitable, by white settlers. Their broad plains, fertile valleys, and rich mountain glens were swarming with hordes of cruel and bloodthirsty savages, who made war on each other and killed and tortured without mercy the few intrepid traders and hunters who had the misfortune to fall in their way. The same is true of the countries south—Colorado, New Mexico, Arizona, etc. With little exception, save here and there, where the vanguard of civilization had daringly planted her outposts, it was an unexplored and trackless waste, a supposed uninhabitable desert.

It has been said that there is now no desert, and we sometimes hear the question: "Where is the great American Desert?" It is true that geography has buried it—American progress and enterprise have ignored it, and the railroad era has eclipsed it, but we who have traversed that long and wondrous track remember well the long stretches of tawny sands—the misty desert sands of the Humboldt.

However, here, amid that which was once deemed a vast wilderness of desert, fertile spots are found, and wherever found, there has industry and enterprise flung out her royal signal—farms are cultivated and homes and hamlets lend an air of beauty to the scene—so that, literally, "The desert is made to blossom as the rose." All along the shining track of the railroads, civilization has planted her invincible banner. Cities, towns and villages—not the mirage of the desert, but flourishing and prosperous communities, peopled by the very nerve and sinew of the land, rise upon the misty air of the aforetime interminable desert and unexplored centre land of the continent, the region which was for ages, for aught history or tradition tells us, the domain of the savage, the primeval home and haunt of swarms of buffalo, roving bands of wild horses, and countless bear, deer, antelope, elk, and many other species of wild animals peculiar to the climate. But with the first shriek of the mysterious monster, the iron horse, and as the wave of civilization sweeps onward, we see them vanishing like the dusky phantoms of a dream. With sullen and reluctant step the red brethren fall back before the advance of the white man. Their dusky figures are dimly seen through the clouds of dust, arising from the herds of buffalo, wild horses and the myriad animals who like themselves are seeking escape and fleeing to the uttermost parts of the continent. On their familiar but now deserted hunting grounds, and along the margins of their beloved rivers, the white man has made homes, and built splendid cities and turned the soil of the green plain, which, yielding its weight of golden treasures now bend in the passing breeze. There, too, are schools, colleges and churches, for wherever "the course of empire takes its way," there the Christian religion, like the quenchless light of the eternal stars, sheds its harmonizing and Christ-like influence.

Judging by the past rate of their decrease—the Indian, like the Aztecs of Mexico, will soon be numbered among the extinct races. He has fulfilled his destiny, and as he stands on his last refuge with his handful of followers, gazing over his once grand and undisputed possessions, we are reminded of the eloquent speech of Iron Bull, chief of the Crows, who with a number of his tribe witnessed the driving of the last spike of the Northern Pacific Railroad. To him was given the honor of presenting the spike to be used on the occasion. His speech, on being interpreted, was as follows:

"This is the last of it—this is the last thing for me to do. I am glad to see you here, and I hope my people of the Crow nation are glad to see you, too. There is a meaning in my part of the ceremony, and I understand it. We have reached the end of our *regimé* and a new one has come. The end of our lives, too, is near at hand. The days of my people are also numbered—already they are dropping off like the last rays of sunlight which hang on the western sky. Of our once powerful nation, there are now but a few left, only just a little handful, and we, too, will soon be gone. After the savage, though, has given way to civilization, the whites will come, they will enjoy the same bright skies, the same glad sunshine, the beauteous mountains, lakes and rills where once we delighted so to roam. They will probably live in it, populate it with the flowers of their race, but will they forever remain in undisputed possession of this grand domain? Who knows but what some race, at present unknown to them, will make its appearance and overpower and take away the land from them, too. Then, as the last chief of the pale face nation stands before the conqueror, will he bid him welcome to his all, to his home, to his life, to his very soul, with more earnestness and as much sincerity as his red brother welcomes him now. I am glad to see you here, I am perfectly willing to yield to the advance of the higher and better civilization; the iron horse will now have a free field to itself, the Indian and Indian pony cannot hope to further roam as in the past, where such a civilizer penetrates. To you, President Villard, to you and your associates of the Northern Pacific road, Iron Bull, Chief of the Crows, presents this spike, with the hope that you will drive it well home, and thus have it bind the hearts of your red brethren to you and your enterprise, as closely and as firmly as it binds your ties of steel, the one to the other."

THE AGE OF GOLD.

The golden age dawned with its discovery in California in 1848, since that time the auriferous metal has been found in the larger portion of the Pacific and northern countries. It has served as a rapid civilizer and means of opening up and developing those hitherto seemingly inaccessible countries. It lured by its glittering power unnumbered hosts from their comfortable homes and the charms of society, to brave dangers' and hostilities in the rude borders of untried savage wilds. The growth and development of those countries has been something bordering on the magical. Had it not been for gold, the glittering phantom, the tardy march of civilization might have been ages in accomplishing what a comparatively few short years have done. Does it not then appear that the age of gold has fulfilled its mission? Lo, the land is peopled—everywhere is written the "march of empire!"

DECREASE OF MINING.

Many of the mines—particularly in the rich surface and placer regions, have been worked out and abandoned. Towns which sprang up in the short space of a few years, and which grew and developed into active and prominent business places, are now almost abandoned.

How different their appearance now, contrasted with those early days! Those now abandoned mining camps were then scenes of activity, energy and prosperity, with their long lines of sluice boxes threading their way through the yellow "diggings" and bands of busy miners picking and shoveling in the coveted dust. From the rude cabins which dotted every hill, the blue smoke of the pine knots curling upward, told that they were occupied. Fine hotels and neat cottages and substantial business houses occupied the "main street" of the camp. The sight of these old deserted camps, wrecked dwellings, and cabins mouldering into ruin, and the general air of silence, and—death, brings up a mournful train of thought. To one whose life and soul, and whose very existence was a part of these busy scenes, the once familiar but now wrecked dwellings, bring a feeling akin to looking on the face of a dead friend. It is an uncomfortable sensation, and though the sight of the grand old mountains, always unchanged, sublime and familiar, bring to the heart a feeling of pleasure, we would fain hasten our steps and leave a scene so full of wreck, desertion and decay.

Quartz and hydraulic mining have taken the place of the old methods, and in many places this process of mining is carried on with success and profit. Many towns and camps have retained much of their early prosperity, and along the foothills or lower Sierra, below the snow line, other industries have claimed the attention of the people. This region is better adapted to the growth of some particular kinds of fruit than the valleys. Apples, peaches and many other varieties of fruit, possess a finer flavor, and it is also highly adapted to the cultivation of the vine. Stock is raised to some extent among the foothills, and permanent homes and prosperous communities abound.

WHEAT GROWING.

Though gold was the grand incentive that lured the early emigrants to the Pacific Coast, many of whom found it in almost exhaustless plenty, but all found something better. They found a country whose genial atmosphere rivals the famed Arcadia, a land whose wealth of soil and blending of rare climatic influences is equalled by few and excelled by none—a country fitted in its natural conditions for the homes of the proudest race of earth. From the restless and exciting thirst for gold, and its feverish and phantom-like chase, they turned their attention to the cultivation of the rich and fertile soil. The yield was enormous, and they soon acquired from this unlooked-for source, wealth and prosperity, and with it contentment, and California in the brief period of thirty years has developed into one of the most important wheat-growing countries in the world. In 1880 the wheat crop was worth over fifty million dollars.

To the eye of the 'Easterner and those unaccustomed to the large grain fields, such as are met with in Sacramento, Colusa, San Joaquin and other counties, the sight is one worthy of attention. It is no uncommon thing here to see thousands of acres owned and cultivated by one man. The buildings of the farm comprise in themselves a considerable village, being the residence occupied by the family, the cottages for the workmen, huge barns, stables, sheds, blacksmith shop, windmill and tank house, and various outbuildings. To the eye of the traveler, as he journeys over the long, level plain, these ranches present the appearance of a stiring village, more paticularly if the season is harvest and the hour noon. Several "headers" and a thresher are usually employed, with their necessary complement of men, horses and mules. If within a mile or so of the house, they repair thither for their meals, and as they file toward the house, men and animals present the appearance of a regiment of soldiery. Generally, however, a cook-house on wheels is provided, which accompanies them night and day; water is hauled in huge tanks and the company camps wherever night overtakes them, in the midst of thousands of acres of yellow grain waving in the wind. Wrapping themselves in their blankets they camp under the clear sky, with no fear of rain or chilling dews to disturb health or comfort. Immense stacks of wheat, cut, threshed and in the sack, at intervals over all the broad field, tell where "the battle raged the fiercest." But the custom of farming immense tracts of land by a few individuals has its serious objections. It is a species of monopoly that is fast growing into disfavor, and in many places, disuse. While it has, in years past, been the means of enriching the few, it has also retarded the growth of communities in preventing thousands of families, in moderate circumstances, from obtaining homes in desirable locations, thereby rendering society little more than a name. Where a neighborhood comprises only a few families, and these are scattered over a vast extent of country, each farm encompassing several miles, little social intercourse is possible. Schools are few and far between, and churches still more rare. Except for the pleasure of money-getting and the power of wealth, this style of farming has few attractions, especially to the cultured and refined, and those who love the society of their fellow beings.

Some years ago, a lady, accomplished and refined, who had been reared in the kindly and social atmosphere of the Eastern states, married a wealthy rancher of one of our wheat raising counties, who owned and cultivated several thousand acres of fine land. He took his young bride to his fine but lonely estate, which was to him his only world. How was it with her? Accustomed to the attractions of society, she soon wearied of the monotonous hum-drum life of a large ranch, of its confinement and loneliness, and became discontented, repining for home and the old life. In a few years she lost all interest in her surroundings; her mind, impaired, drifted into a settled melancholy; from that she became a raving maniac, and when I heard her mournful story from the lips of a friend, she was in the asylum for the insane at Stockton.

SMALL FARMING.

But it may now be said of the wheat raising mania in California that it has reached its fever heat and subsided; other industries as lucrative have sprung up, many of which will come under the head of "small farming." In many counties, both northern and southern, large tracts of land have been divided and laid out in small subdivisions and sold to persons desirous of engaging in fruit-raising, bee-keeping and other industries, thus insuring homes to families of moderate means and building up communities of thrift, beauty and prosperity.

In many of the southern counties the culture of the orange, lemon, olive, fig and the vine are taking the precedence in small farming. In the central and northern counties, viniculture has taken a prominent position among the new industries, a large percentage of the land in the State being peculiarly adapted to the growth of the vine.

NAPA COUNTY.

Among the counties which are taking a front rank in this rapidly increasing industry, we cite Napa County. We mention this county more particularly because it is *our* county; for many years our home has nestled among its beautiful vales and mountains, and we know whereof we speak. More than a passing reference is due to this charming and attractive county which, irregular in shape, consists of beautiful valleys divided by mountainous ranges. The valley of Napa, which is the principal one, is some thirty-five miles in length, with a width varying from one mile at the northern end to five at the southern; through its entire length flows the lovely river of Napa, into which empty numerous tributaries. The soil is peculiarly adapted to the growth of the vine and the various semi-tropical and temperate fruits. The climate is cool, and at the southern extremity, subject to fogs. The principal town, also the county seat, is Napa, noted for its attractive residences, beautiful gardens, and fine location. Two daily and two weekly papers are published here. The Napa State Asylum for the Insane, located in the suburbs of the town on a sightly eminence, is an object of special interest. The mass of buildings, stupendous and imposing in appearance, are among the finest in the State. Seen at a distance, this colossal structure, with its massive wings, domes and towers, presents a magnificent appearance. It was built at a cost of $1,500,000, and accommodates from 600 to 800 patients.

Another noteworthy institution is the newly finished "Veterans' Home," situated nine miles from the town of Napa. The Napa Valley Railroad runs almost the whole length of the valley, and terminates at Calistoga, near the upper end, twenty-seven miles from Napa. [The San Francisco and Clear Lake Railroad, now being built, is designed to run from Napa through a portion of the valley, and crossing, takes its way into Lake County.]

Along the line of the Valley Railroad, are numerous towns and pleasant villages, the most noted, the most attractive and most prosperous being, St. Helena, eighteen miles from Napa. In this vicinity, and in fact through the entire valley, the vine-growing industry has supplanted that of wheat growing. Large grain farms have been divided into small tracts of from fifteen to twenty acres and upward, and have been planted in vines, orchards, hop yards, etc. The town itself is a charming and busy centre of activity, situated as it is, in a rich vine growing district, with its numerous wine cellars, elegant residences, schools, churches, etc., and surrounded by lovely suburban villas and beautiful homes embowered by tree and vine. The fact that two semi-weekly papers are published here, both well established and doing a flourishing business, is proof of the prosperity of the place, the surrounding country, and the energetic character of its citizens. In 1880 the wine product alone, of Napa County, was 2,867,250 gallons, and there are fifty-one wine cellars in the county.

Besides its social and home-like attractions, it presents to the tourist and the health-seeker, various popular and inviting resorts, and points of interest. There are in the vicinity of St. Helena, the Crystal Springs and the White Sulphur Springs, also the Geysers, which have for years enjoyed enviable fame. The noted Petrified Forest is distant about fourteen miles, and on the west, for miles, runs the beautiful evergreen "Howell Mountain." Circling its green sides from end to end of the entire chain, is the magical climatic wonder, the thermal or semi-tropical belt. Above the reach of the fog, and humid, chilling atmosphere of the valleys, and out of the reach of frost, it possesses more and greater attractions as a place of residence, than are to be found in almost any other locality. Like many another hidden treasure of this strange land of wonders, its advantages were, for many years, overlooked; now, however, it is being rapidly settled up by those who wish to engage in fruit raising and the cultivation of the vine. "Small farming" is not only engaging the attention of that class of immigrants who seek California with a view of settling, and building up comfortable and pleasant homes, but also of the princely "ranchers," many of whom have become weary of the anxieties, debts and uncertainties attending the farming of an immense tract of land, which, with all its show and apparent wealth, is in many instances devoid of home and comfort. Many, too, have become broken in fortune in a single season of drouth, through becoming involved in debt and paying enormous interest on borrowed money. To those who love the cultivation of the vine, with its luscious grapes, and the various fruits of the semi-tropical and temperate climate, and also of berries and small fruits of every variety, who love to plant and watch the unfolding of the varied gems of the floral kingdom—all which contribute to the beauty and necessities of a home—to these, small farming possesses many attractions. Thirty or forty acres in the valley or on the hill-sides, cleared and in bearing vines, fruits, etc., will insure to its possessor comfort, plenty, peace and health, and with grapes selling at the present rates, from $25 to $35 per ton, according to variety, will, in the end, bring a more satisfactory income than a large wheat farm of several hundred acres.

California has, and justly, been called "The Italy of America." Her skies have been compared to those of Italy, Spain, Greece and Palestine. The assertion is well founded from the variety of her productions and the fascinating glory of her climate. In many favored sections the approach of winter is scarcely observable, save for the falling of the leaves and the green grass carpeting mountain and vale. Winter is an almost uninterrupted spring.

As an illustration, we cite with pleasure "our own little world," which is situated in the Thermal Belt on the green slope of the beautiful mountain previously mentioned. Although it is now the 6th of January, midwinter in the Eastern States, we have scarcely yet felt a breath of king frost. The vines at my porch, madeira, rose, climatis, honeysuckle, passion, etc., are as green as in midsummer. The flowers are still in bloom, roses, pinks, pansies, verbenas, myrtle, and other varieties. I have ten or twelve varieties of geraniums, all of which are uninjured by frost. In the garden, raspberries of the Cuthbert variety are still blooming and bearing. On Christmas day I gathered a quantity—they were full-sized, red and juicy. On the grape vines a few tardy bunches of the second crop still linger as though loth to bid farewell to autumn. The ground is covered with green grass, and the lovely manzanita, with its beautiful waxen flowers, is in full bloom; add to this, the surrounding evergreen forest, is made more fresh and perfect by the recent rains. In this we have presented a picture—and a true one, of "The Italy of America."

SAN FRANCISCO IN 1884.

San Francisco in 1884, as in early days, when the wealth of the mines poured in seemingly endless profusion into the grand nucleus of trade and commerce of the Pacific Coast, so now the products of the soil and numberless industries, a far more substantial source of wealth gravitates to that suburb centre. Steamers, barges and scows on the broad rivers bear outward to the bay, fruits "corn and wine," and the numberless productions of the country, and the numerous lines of railroads tapping the rich arteries of the interior, all laden with products of the soil and the mines, glide onward and converge at the same point. A visit to the Bay City toward the close of 1883, and we beheld her in all her magnificence and splendor—truly, "A city that is set on a hill cannot be hid!" But what a wonderful transformation since the time when a stranger I first set foot on her glittering sands nearly thirty years ago! No longer are the hills covered with long strings of insignificant and rambling shanties, thrown together to supply the immediate and pressing demand, for these have given place to magnificent and palatial mansions and imposing blocks of granite, and looking from the bay as we steam toward the shore, we see the golden shafts of sunlight glancing over towers, domes, temples and minarets—in the words of a popular writer "A city that rivals the cities of the East in splendor and magnificence and excels them in wealth." The hills in many places have been cut down to fill up the hollows and the shallow margin of the bay, and over this made land a large part of the best of the city is built. Little does the stranger surmise as he treads the crowded thoroughfares of this part of the city, that the eager multitude daily passes up and down over places where the green waves of the bay once rolled in undisturbed serenity.

Mills and factories, for the manufacture of the various productions of the State, have been in successful operation for many years; every branch of industry is here represented, every business has its headquarters here. Around the rim of the beautiful bay that almost encircles the peninsula on which the city is situated, is a forest of shipping. Through the magnificent Golden Gate steamers and vessels of every description are arriving from all parts of the world, and moored at the numerous wharves, and riding at anchor on the bay, are the various "crafts of the sea," taking in freight. Wheat, flour, fruits and wine are among the principal articles of export. An immense trade is carried on with China, Japan, the islands of the Pacific, Great Britain, South America, the Eastern States, and many other countries.

The lapse of years has not changed many of the peculiar features of this essentially cosmopolitan city. The population, which is at present estimated at about 330,000, is composed of representatives from all parts of the world, and it is without doubt partly owing to this fact that there are many features connected with it of more than ordinary interest, even for a city of its natural advantages and commercial importance.

Strangers are invariably directed to Woodward's Gardens, which, with their underground aquarium department, beautiful plants and flowers and innumerable curiosities, are well worth a day's sojourn in the city, to visit.

The street cars are constantly filled with eager sight-seers going to this popular resort. To those who have not been accustomed to the "cable cars," the wonderful wire-rope railroads, moving without the slightest visible propelling power, gliding with their loads of passengers straight up and down hills, over which many of the streets of San Francisco run, the sight is a novel one.

In the environs of the city are many charming resorts and splendid drives; the Cliff House, famous for its Seal Rock, where abound those curious specimens of the deep; Golden Gate Park and the delightful drive to it along the bay shore, with a view of the Golden Gate and the ocean beyond, the broad bay, and numerous islands, the ocean vessels, under full sail and steam, ploughing the dancing waves or riding at anchor on the bosom of the deep.

Golden Gate, the grand entrance to the harbor and bay within, is a beautiful strait six miles long by one mile wide. It is said that when viewed from the east, at sunset, the effect is sublime. It then is really a gate of gold in a crimson setting, with the changing tints of sunset reflecting and radiating on the vast expanse of water beyond.

AND THE SEA.

There's a land whose fair borders are washed by a sea,
    A sea whose broad bosom is—peace.
'Tis a clime of our earth, but its glittering strand
Slopes down from a mountain chain wondrously grand,
    Where the region of Empire doth cease;
And Empire sits there, by the far reaching sea,
    With her feet in the beautiful sea.

Her footprints we've seen on the desolate plain
    Where she trailed her white robes thro' the vast
Burning sands and deep rivers—now cities abound,
Which arose at the wave of her magical wand.
    But the limit of Empire is cast,
And she sits on the land that is washed by the sea,
    The waves of the west-going sea.

And the land that she reached at the last is the best;
    For its mountains bear treasures of gold,
And the green sweeping plains and sweet vales seemed to woo
The homes that now greet us; and wandering through
    Are the rivers, whose murmuring waters doth roll,
And mingle and merge with the waves of the sea,
    The waves of the shimmering sea.

The vales breathe of spices and odorous bloom:
    The orange, the fig and the vine;
And fields of rich verdure spread inland and wide,
Whose wealth is borne out on the far flowing tide,
    To the strand whose broad margin is lined
With the vessels that freighted are bound for the sea,
    The ships that sail over the sea.

The Queen of the West, like a siren of old,
    Sits throned on her radiant hills,
In splendor and wealth. Her temples and towers
Rise grand from the sea, in their pride and their power,
    And the land with her praises is filled—
And outward she looks to the gate that is gold,
Thro' which ages and ages the billows have rolled,
    They bear on their breast to the sea—
In the barks that sail out to the Orient climes,
   The treasure and wealth of the Queen of the West,
    The bride of the beautiful sea.

THE END.

www.ingramcontent.com/pod-product-compliance
Lightning Source LLC
Chambersburg PA
CBHW032142160426

43197CB00008B/752